Other titles
by
Corey Hamilton

Keep Left
Society's Grip
Exit Is A Safe Place
No One Shall Be Spared
Open Up
Mash Notes
Mash Notes: vol 2
Lonely Night Songs
2 Days
Unhyped
Time Marches On
Thirty Three
VI
What If?
Magic Bus
How I Remember It
Cease & Desist
Sensible Shoes
Do Not Ever Have Any Good Ideas
DNA
I Am NOT With The Band
Wedge Politics
My Side Project

Too Personal

Copyright © 2008 Corey Hamilton

All rights reserved. No part of this book may be reproduced or transmitted in any form or by any means, graphic, mechanical or electronic, including photocopying and recording, or by any information storage or retrieval system without written permission from the publisher, except for brief passages quoted in review.

Library and Archives Canada Cataloguing in Publication

Hamilton, Coery, 1971-
   Too personal / Corey Hamilton.

Poems.
ISBN 978-0-9697305-9-0

   I. Title.

PS8565.A5347T66 2008   C811'.54   C2008-901414-6

Front, back cover photographs of the author as well as photographs on pages 138 to 162 and page 411 all taken by Corey Hamilton © 2008.

Painting used on the front and back cover "Security Blanket", detail 2005, oil on canvas, 48 x 60 in. © Corey Hamilton.

Book layout and design by Corey Hamilton.

First Printing

Published by Dramatic Situations
         P.O. Box 696
         Edmonton, AB
         T5J 2L4
         CANADA
www.dramaticsituations.com

Too Personal

Corey Hamilton

F.Y.I.

This book was compiled in the same manner as my fifth book called, "Open Up".

The poetry was written from sometime just before December 31, 2004 and ends february 19, 2008. Pages 1 to 26 are "left overs" from "Open Up", "Mash Notes" and "Mash Notes: Vol 2". Pages 27 to 419 are poems number 1326 to 1600, inclusive. The whole book is done in chronological order so you get a sort of "diary" effect.

The poetry on pages 138 to 162 were written from August 19, 2006 to August 20, 2006. Each piece on these pages were about the photograph on the same page and were meant to be published in a full colour poetry and photography book called "25 Days". The "25 Days" project was basically this, I would take pictures on one roll of film per day and then I would write a poem about one photograph from each roll. Due to unforeseen costs "25 Days" was never published. I have included black and white reproductions of each image so you can understand what the poem was about. The technical information for the "25 Days" project can be found on page number 421 at the back of this book.

The bulk of this book is gloomy but ends on (what I feel is) a positive note. I had a blast compiling this. I hope you have just as good a time reading this.

Enjoy!

#1782

RE-INTRODUCTION

Looking at
My body of work
And how I justify pointing out
Other people's flaws
By pointing out my flaws
Just shows an even bigger flaw
In my logic and
Not to mention myself

That being said
I do not wish
To censor myself
But when my private
Becomes our public
I would like to apologize
For being judgmental
And for not pointing out sooner
That all who I have criticized
Who are closer to me
Than the common riff raff
Have good intentions
And even better hearts
And I sincerely hope
That you accept
My humble apology
For not pointing out
Your good intentions
And even better hearts
Before I pointed out
Your flaws

#1295

Next Spring

Now I'm whacked out on codeine
Trying to protect myself
From this raging migraine
It is not what I want
But it will have to do
I will crawl into all of the fissures
And cracks of Mount Robson
To hide from my dreams of you
Maybe they'll find me next spring
Looking like the uni-bomber
Or maybe rotten from death's grip
From rotting the whole winter
Where no one found me
Until I rolled myself out
And down the side of the mountain
Leaving a trail of rotten flesh
The whole damn way down
Dropping bombs
The whole way down
On shinning cities
On shinning people
No matter how clean
I will still drop bombs
On myself too
The codeine has finally worn off
And I am left wondering
What the hell I just wrote

#1300

Take It Back

I will take a pass
And see you in the new year
When nothing changes
When my tears still run
Because a quarter
Doesn't even get you a phone call
I ache
All over
I am touched by your words
I am offended by your actions
But we won't talk about it
I know what I will be doing
In two weeks
Thinking about how
We never even got started
Or
We finished
Just as we got started
And
I don't know about you
But I have to make small talk
And try to start over
With someone else
I never have the right words
To say
To write
To think
So I will walk away from it all
Because
I will have to take another pass
Wondering why I never grow?
If a tree doesn't fall
In a forest
Does anyone see it grow?

If I don't fall
In a city
Does anyone see me go?
Probably not

Probably not

#1301

Poison

You drink
You smoke
You fuck
You snort
You pose naked
For me
And my camera
You have a hard time
Making enemies
And that's why I like you
The chances are like
A winning lottery ticket
The chances of you
Calling me
One more time
You drink
You smoke
You fuck
(At least I think you do)
You snort
Or I know now
You used to snort
And now that you are cleaner
I like you more
I got up early
To check my lottery ticket
Another loser
I got up early
To write about you calling me
And you still haven't
Another loser

#1303

A Smile A Week

Every week I see her
And I sensed an awkwardness
From her
The very first time I saw her
I thought that she was the cutest
Woman I had seen in ages
But I sensed her awkwardness
But I still made her smile
And I saw her top and bottom retainers
And heard her uncomfortable english
I can't tell if she is from
The Philippines or Singapore
I would ask
But I don't want to pry
But I felt bad for her
Maybe she came from another country
And has screwed up teeth
And has a hard time with the language
And she gets paid to clean up after
White pigs like me
So I am determined
So determined
To make her smile
Whenever I see her
Just to make her feel welcome
By someone here
I don't feel sorry for her
I feel sorry for the people
Who don't see her smile
Like I do
Every week

#1304

A Touch Of Sorrow

You have your baby
Growing inside you
And him to hold your hand
I have a silent phone
Next to mine
Everyone I know
Is attached
To everyone else I know
When I was younger
I never looked twice
At your kind
And now that I am older
And see the river
Getting farther away
In my rearview mirror
I know
Or at least
I think I know
My time has passed me by
Which way do you go
When I ask you out?
The other
Which way do you go
When he asks you out?
His way
You never have time for me
But you have all of the time in the world
For the pretty ones
How do you think
That makes me feel
When I found out?
For I was bound to find out
A touch of sorrow

A touch of anger
A touch of bitter
At no touch at all
I hate
Going on like this
But I do anyways
I stumble around
Aimlessly
Until I run into something
Something different
But most of the time
I can tell what is going
To happen
Long before it happens
And when it does happen
It is almost always
A major let down
When I called you
And you told me
That your girl
Is going to have a baby
It caught me off guard
And it was to me
A touch of sorrow
A touch of anger
A touch of bitter
At the end of a love scene
For you
And the end of a war zone
For me

#1305

Deeper Than You

It is minus 23 outside
Where everyone is going somewhere
To do something
Everyone except me that is
So which way will you have me
If you won't have him?
Or should I say
Except me
Except me that is
My food was bought by my folks
My drugs are mostly samples
I owe friends money
Your bride is having your child
And I should be happy?
People tell me my work is great
But they won't put their name on it
Or won't put their money down
I can't live on or off of praise
The more praise I get
The more I feel insulted
This has been happening lately
Everyone is going somewhere
To ring in a new one
And me?
Home alone writing
I should be happy eh?
I <u>should</u> be happy.

this piece was written at 7:09 PM
on December 31, 2004
in Edmonton

#1307

David

I had a dream last night
About Michelangelo's sculpture
"David"
About how much damage
Is being done to it
By the environment
I woke up sad
Thinking that such a great piece of art
I have never seen up close
Is "dying" slowly
I will probably never see "David"
In my lifetime
And if I do
He may be in seclusion
And I may not be able to breathe
The same air as him
All this sadness
Over a dream
I am running from my dream
About "David"
Because the amount of work
Put into "David" baffles me
And the sadness
Put out by my dream
Baffles me too

#1309

Beast Of Burden

High on the hog
I need something to smoke
(And I don't mean cigarettes)
I need something to drink
(And I don't mean soda pop)
Looks as if
I can't stop
This remote control ride
This no feeling show
This "I wish I was on the highway"
But I know I am not
They want me poor
They want me to break
To die
So I won't be a burden
This is an anthology
Of desperation
Of desolation
Sooner or later
I will fly
And drop bombs
On my skeptics
On my critics
On my leaches
Who are and have been
High on the hog
Living off of my somethings
Down here
Searching for something
To put me on the highway
Patience,
Be patient.

#1310

Sailing Away

If one day
You see me sailing away
In a crowd
Be kind
And lend a helping hand
So I don't sail off
Of this square earth
I will take my sins
And wash them in the creek
And hope goodness
Comes out of it
So I can repay
All I have sinned against
And feel good about myself
Once more
Does all of the little bad
One does
Add up
To one big terrible?
Does all of the little good
One does
Add up
To one big wonderful?
I don't know the answers
To either of these questions
I try to be good to myself
And those around me
And I hope that it does add up
To something so positive
I won't have to worry
About the negative
But I am still skeptical
As I am still sailing away

#1311

New Tattoo

I lie to you
About my scarring
I do to myself
Because it costs money
And I have so little
Money
And so many scars already
I feel terrible
And hope
That something goes my way
So I can make reparations
Some day I will die
After you have given me your hand
And with all of the regret
Of the third world
And all of the lies
Of the western world
I will die
Never knowing honesty
Until it is a scar on my body
To match the rest on the outside
And to match the rest on the inside

#1313

Not Impressed

I looked out of my kitchen window
Thinking the person by the van outside
Was my Dad
He wasn't my Dad
It was a man hugging a woman
The man had his hands around her
While the woman looked straight ahead
With a dead face
And hands at her side
The man released her and looked at her
Dead face
And hugged her again
He finished
And she got into her van
And drove off
All the while looking straight ahead
With a dead face
The man stood on the sidewalk
Looking at her
Almost like he was hoping that
She would look back and wave
She didn't
And he crawled back into his home

One night
In a bar near my home
I was sitting inside by myself
When a pretty woman
Asked me if the seat on the right
Was taken
I was trying to be friendly and funny
I said, "Yes, by you."
She scowled at me and left
She then sat alone in a booth by herself
Scowling at me
Recently I was out with a friend
And I saw her again

I wondered if she would scowl at me
She didn't
She looked me in the eyes and smiled
A gorgeous smile
I responded with a dead face
And then turned away
I find it harder
To be a nice guy all of the time
Than to be an asshole
An asshole with a dead face

Hugging man should have gotten the drift
And so should have my new scowling female "Friend"
The woman who didn't want a hug
For whatever reason
And myself who didn't like getting scowled at
For whatever reason
We were both
Not
Impressed

#1314

Down And Again

Every time you breathe
You steal a naked piece of me
And happiness is tied
To those pieces
And happiness is a movie now
Not an emotional state
Emotional states always sink
Down and down
Again and again
The jukebox sings its bandaid song
Again and again
Down and down
Where you eventually
Won't find me ever again
How's that Grandpa H.?
When you gave me your hand
I will know I have finally won
Never
Again and again
Down and down
Where nothing is in the grass
But a short story I started
Years ago
When I was much younger
Thinking that I could conquer that story
But knowing deep down inside
I never would
Even if I finished it
I never would conquer it
Again and again
Down and down
But that is all I can write
For now
Because my bus is coming

So I have to go
Down and again

See The Light

I whisper when I tell the truth
And I yell when I lie
Maybe that's why
I am
Always getting into trouble
When what I really want to say
Is locked up tight
Between these lines
I could burn you alive
But martyrs live forever
I used to live in a river
But I was dragged up
To be with you
I used to sleep under a rock
But you turned it over
Like a new leaf
And exposed me to the light
Just like you and yours
I like the shadows
But I guess
Sooner or later
We all get exposed
Whether we want to or not
The tears
That are in my eyes
Will dry
Sooner or later
They will dry
Dreams
Are so close
But seem so far away
From my light
And my whisper voice
That I may cry

Yet again
Because there is always "hell"
In hello
And there is always "good"
In goodbye
It should be the opposite
But it isn't
And now I know
You are the everything

#1317

Him Smile

I hope that my Grandfather died smiling
Knowing how much he made others around
Him smile
I will never know
And I am not sure
If I have ever grown
Since then
How come some are tortured for years
And still smile meekly
The last time you see them
It was the middle of winter
That I last saw him
And I have been lost
Ever since
Because all of the white and black boys and girls
Don't care
And all of the aboriginals are drunk
Around here
And they only want my money or empties
Or better yet, both
I have chosen to believe he was happy
But I know deep down inside
He wore his regret
Like a scarlet letter
In the center of his chest
At least he made me happy
Every time I saw him smile

#1318

I have got two pieces of paper left
(Including the one I am writing on)
In this whole place
So I guess
I had better pull up my anchor
And do some good for once
Yesterday I cried alot
In the morning
About missing my Grandfather
Who has been dead now
For almost exactly 15 years
Sad day
It could be worse
I could be spilt beer
On the floor
Of some shitty bar
And people are stepping all over me
No thank you
That is not enough for me
The next day will be better
I hope
I drop my anchor
In this place I am in
And do some more
Of my writing
Hoping that you will notice me
And it won't matter
How many pieces of paper
I have left
I want you to touch me
And I want to be brave enough
To return the favor
It is a nice dream
But I know
Where this is going
Even though my anchor

Isn't letting me go very far
Because
Now I have
One piece of paper left
So I had better make it good

#1320

Stalker Being Stalked

Why do you follow me?
What is it you wanted?
Are you waiting for me to fall?
Or take a fall for you?
Or fall head over heals
Falling over you?
The last question you ever asked me was
"Where are you?"
The same place I have been for years
Idiot
You lost track of me
Then you ask me,
You have the nerve to ask me
Where I am?
Shit
How stupid can one get?
Stop following me!
I don't want any part
Of you and your immaturity
Or of your immature, jealous boyfriend
Get it?
Got it?
Good.
Note to self
The next woman/girl who smiles at you
Don't trust
I have a male friend who says,
"Never trust a girl who says that
She is on the pill."
Shit
I have a hard time trusting
Any girl
Let alone one on or off of the pill
Shit

Again
I am going to get off topic again
Again
I remember getting up early with you
Around 6AM on a Saturday morning
To play pool at a nearby pool hall
And then playing pool for hours
You used to get angry at me
For calling you "Pool Shark"
And then the two of us going for breakfast
At a nearby cafe
That was owned by a Chinese couple
Who made the best milkshakes
Both places are gone now
And so are you
But the questions still haunt me
Visions of you haunt me
And now it feels as if
The stalker
Is being stalked

#1321

A Hundred Years Or More

A hundred years
And a hundred more
I have been under the radar
Wondering when that magic wand
Would touch my shoulders and head
Last night I could only sleep
For 20 minutes at a time
Before nightmares woke me
If there is a god
He hates you
For burning me
Even though god only knows
That I was meant for burning too
Is that all I am good for?
A spark
To burn my work with?

#1322

Say Yes To Me

It was a cautious display
Of hands
At first
Now it is late night calls
That just upset me
And leave me not wanting
To be around here anymore
Feeling like you will never say yes
To me
The holes in your plan
Are not visible to my eye
Maybe I should move on
And keep you private
But it should be me
And not him
Such a mess I am in
A complacent mess
I know when I am wrong
And I damn well know when I am right
But right now
I have a silent phone
And an even more silent heart
Not wanting to rock the boat
Too much
But enough to get noticed
But enough
But enough
But enough already
And say yes to me
You didn't
You don't
And you won't
I'll see you when
It doesn't sting as much

It is always cautious with me
And even more cautious with you
Dealing with me
Dealing with me
Dealt with you
And move on
Another day more
In this solitary world
Of mine

#1326

What Can I Say?

Don't you call my name
When months have passed
And you've ignored me
Calling your name
Is that what you would call it?
What did you mean
When you said that it didn't work out
Between us?
He never said that
I am in the same direction
As him
And yet you snub me
How am I supposed to feel?
They said that life would be different
Once I graduated from high school
I discovered that it never changed
Nothing ever changes
"What are we,
Just monkeys?"
She asked me
I didn't really know what to say
But that I think some people are
Just monkeys
I am so tired of the monkeys
I am so tired of this study
In human response
If you aren't a monkey
Then you are a baby
And if you aren't a baby
Then you are a baby monkey
When I am snubbed
Time stands still
And I am left feeling
Like I don't know any language on Earth
Is this all just a test?
If so,
Am I failing miserably

Next time I see you
Watch your ass
I am tired of telling people
To watch their ass
When I am busy
Protecting mine
Don't bring that in here!
Why?
Because you are not wanted
In here
With that attitude
Why?
Because we are tired of you
And your monkey business
I am tired of giving
People the benefit
Of the doubt
When they have little or no respect
For me
Maybe I shouldn't worry about this
But I do
You are fully responsible
For my loneliness
For my guilt
For my shame
For my anger
For my despair
And for the rain
On what is supposed to be
My sunny day
You don't know what it is like
To be constantly pushed around
The loneliness
The guilt
The shame
The anger
The despair
And the rain
On what is supposed to be
My sunny day
Last night I had a nightmare
That one of my good friends

Who is currently the friendliest person
In my life
Turned into a mean spirited jerk
One day
Instead of giving me a ride
When I lived on the way
He left me in minus 30 degree weather
I hope that this isn't an omen
I hope that I haven't pushed him
Too far
So that an awful ending
Is now inevitable
I gaze off into space for awhile
Wishing that I could go there
And watch for awhile
Maybe even learn something
About you all
And about myself
Or have I learned enough
About myself
And about you all
I am not calling you again
I am bored of your drivel
I don't want to hear it
We are not friends
If you don't even return my calls
So I guess I <u>haven't</u> heard your drivel in awhile
And now I won't hear it again
Or so it seems
It is getting pretty dark outside
And it is the middle of the day
So here it comes again
All of the rain and fuss
About everyone else
But themselves
You are always right
And I am always wrong
It is impossible to be that way
But here it is
Just the facts
And it is such hard work
Not to piss you off

And it is such hard work
Not to cheat on you
There I said it
I didn't want to
But there it is
Just the facts
And here is something else
You might want to know
The next time we meet
<u>You</u> had better watch your ass
Because I am through watching my own
Around you
I am going to dump on you
The same way you
Dumped, dump and will dump
On me
And see how you like it
<u>You</u> had better watch your ass
Because I won't be watching it anymore
It is just too fat
From your condescending nature
Towards everyone else
And your constant sitting around
On that pedestal you created
The same one that you put yourself on
Thanks for coming
Now don't let the door
Hit your fat ass on the way out
Yes
You heard me
At first I thought I liked you
But now I know
I could never like a snotty snob
Some of my family
Are like that
And I tire quickly
Of hearing them
Of seeing them
Of knowing them
I would rather that a snob
Ignores me
Than talks to me

Or says that they know me
I have tried to keep this clean
But it is very hard
When people who disrespect me
Push me down and around
They disrespect me
Most times for no reason
If I see you on the street
I will cross to the other side
If you confront me
I will disrespect you
And see how you like it
Sometimes I feel guilty
About an eye for an eye
But most times
I would rather cross the street
Than talk nicely
When I would rather
Gouge out your eyeballs when confronted
By you and your snot
You should come and live in my shoes
And see if you would feel
Any different
Than this rant
I ranted on and on about
This or that
Make your choice
You have?
Good.
I know that you will stick by it
And now
I will put my venom
In your veins
And see if you feel
Any different
Than this rant
It is so dark out
And that suits me fine
For when the sun shines
I will feel a little better
But I will still feel like an alien
There

I said it
Just like you
Said it
Only what I said
Was honest about me
And what you said
Was snot to me
Soon I will show you a mirror
And it will crack and break
Under your snot
And I hope
That finally
You will see my light
And you will also see everyone else's light too
And you will finally feel guilty
About your snotty actions

A long time ago I asked
"What can I say?"
Now I know

Now I know

#1327

Fingers And Backs

You point your finger
At me
Knowing full well
I can't write songs
Then you forget about me
Next time we meet
I will pass by you
Like a ghost
Or I will pull a u-turn
And turn my back
On you
The same way
You just did months ago
"Tell your wife and kid
That you blew it again!"
I say to myself
Nothing I have for sale
Is for sale to you or for you
Now I am pointing the finger
At you
With my back
At you

#1328

Today As Me As Ever

Today
In the middle of summer
I fell asleep
With my alarm set to go off
At the first sign of snow
Hopefully
I don't sleep through my alarm
If I do
Promise me that you will
Wake me up
When you have an affair
So I can walk out on you
The way you walked out on me
Sometimes
I don't like my dreams
Because they either
Turn into nightmares
Or never come true
I think of Terry Fox
And wonder what his dreams were
And if he ended up
In the same predicament
As me
The difference would be
He is a hero 25 years after his death
And I am not a hero
Or dead
I am still alive and broke
As ever
And unknown
As ever

As ever

#1329

Can You Hear Me?

Pull up the stakes
Pull up my socks
And get out of Dodge
Never to be seen again
Just heard from once a year
Almost like a myth
I think that I would go
To the country
Where I wouldn't be recognized
Can you hear me?
I can't sleep at night
Anymore
Than you can
For your sins
And for my sins
Yes
I am making a statement
You fool
You made one to me
Now it is my turn
Because in this day and age
You get what you pay for
I got mountains
And you got mole hills
And I still want to move
Maybe a mole hill
Would be more comfortable
For me
Than these under used
Mountains

#1330

What Would Happen If...

What would happen if
I sold out
To you?
Would you treat me like
A slave?
An underling?
A hero?
Or an equal?

What would happen if
I sold out
To you?
Would you treat me
The same?
Or would you
Suck up to me
Or ignore me until the end of time?

So
What would happen if
I sold out
To you?

#1331

Forgetting My Memory

When will my memory fade
And give it
And me
A rest?
I am tired of remembering
Wake me up
When I have forgotten something
For once
Let me forget something
I saw you again
You were with your jealous boyfriend
You made like
You were never in the hospital
The first time we met
I wish I could forget my time too
Wake me up when it snows
And I have forgotten
About the summer
More time drifts away
And my memory gets larger
And my need for stitches
Gets larger too
Please give it a rest
Please give me a rest
Memory
Please fade
And give it
And me a rest

#1332

Her Arms

Come down
This long road with me
And we shall see
What our bones say
And if we wither
In the pale moonlight
Come up
To the top floor with me
Because I am scared
Too scared
To sign
By myself
Even if I should
Go it alone
I can't wait
For a saviour
When I am half dead
Do I have to go it alone
When I know
I will die inside
Her arms
Dust to dust
Ashes to ashes
Rust to rust
Come down
Then up
We'll see
Who laughs the longest
When it is long past
The time to even smile
And is now the time
To come down
From coming up
I will die inside

Her arms

#1333

Work Pain

Falling on deaf ears
Falling on blind eyes
Answers from mute lips
Nothing could be worse
Than nothing from anybody
May I be strong enough
To survive this
Lack of payment
And live to see
Some sort of payment
For my work's pain
For my pain's work

#1334

How many more times
Must I lean into the wind
Hoping it will take me
To a place
Where stars live on forever
And so do all of my dead
Family and friends

#1335

You Tell Me

You tell me to go smaller
And not to do the abstract
And then
You tell me to go bigger
And stay my course
I want to go wherever
Which ever whatever how ever way
The wind takes me
You tell me
"Van Gogh never sold a painting
And now he is an icon."
I think to myself
Yes
But he is dead
By his own hand
Because he never sold a painting
I can relate to Van Gogh
In a small way
In his position
When he was alive
When I am alive
I feel suicide
Course through my veins
I am struggling to get by
And what makes me happy
Doesn't pay the bills
The money is going out
But not coming back in
How many more scars
Do I need
Before I can see myself
Before I can be myself
Before I can be content
With myself

You won't even look at me
What if I was to quit?
Would it even matter?
I would have all of my work
Burned
Burn me
Burning me
Don't tell me to calm down!
If I look serious
It is because this is a serious matter
Fuckwad!
Don't "he should know better" to me
Bitch cakes!
I have been doing this a long enough time
And I am tired of the shit and abuse
I am put through
Yes, I can hear you fucker!
Quit shouting at me!
Or I will go deaf
And that would be horrible
Because I need all of my senses
Just to get by
On an everyday basis
I told you to quit shouting at me!
You don't like my attitude
Well the feeling is mutual
Mutually assured destruction
I gained nothing by being there
I did lose some self esteem though
So I guess I did go smaller
And I stayed my course
So I took a little of both
Best of both worlds?
A little of both
And you lost
And I lost
You lost
But you are not the loser

That's my job
I guess

#1336

Little Things

My younger
More successful artist sister
Asked me why I paint in oils
When acrylics are cheaper
They dry quicker
And aren't as toxic
My answer was simple
I like the colours of oils better
I like that they take longer to dry
So if I make a mistake
I won't have to start over
But the real reason
Is the smell
The smell reminds me
Of a six million dollar man
Paint by numbers kit
That I got for a birthday
It was oils
And now the smell
Brings me back to a time
Where I could escape
The school beatings
By painting
So I am sorry if this is nostalgic
And if I am hurting the environment
But it is the little things like this
That make me happy
And I never want to lose
Anymore little things
Than I have already

#1337

Emily Dickinson's Best Friend

Your ghost
Has me hiding
Inside my art
Inside my work
Work and art
Without a pension plan
I knew you
Wouldn't call
So I know it all
All again
Please tell me
Why I am
To be alone
Friends come and go
And enemies come and stay
So I hide more
And eat less
Write and paint and photograph
More
And bathe less
Read and listen and smell
More
The smell of my oil paints
The sound of Neil Young's voice and guitar
The words of Goethe or Emily Dickinson
Whenever I ask you to call me
I fuck it up somehow
And never hear from you again
It is almost 5 AM
And I have been awake since 2 AM
Thinking that love is hell
And so is being alone so much

#1338

Nope

No feeling alone
No first glance
No first meeting
No first phone call
No first date
No first hug
No first kiss
No sex
No sleeping together
No holding hands
No midnight snacks
No spending every waking moment together
No meeting parents
No big decision to get married
No wedding plans
No decision to have a big or small wedding
No "in sickness and in health"
No "til death do you part"
No placing of ring on finger
No drunk wedding guests we don't know
No big decision to have kids
No kids
No heated arguments
No divorce
No drunken calls at 3 AM on a weeknight
No alimony
No child support
No supervised meetings
No "absence makes the heart grow fonder"
No A.I.D.S.
No bitterness
No upset children
No public displays of anger
No public displays of sadness

No depression
No suicidal thoughts
No feeling alone again
Nope
None of the above

#1339

Till Death Do Us Part

Later on in the day
When I have nothing better to do
I will think
Think of you
And how poorly you treated me
I fought back
And burned you
Now I feel guilty
Wondering if you ever
For a minute
Feel guilty too
I know you
I had pockets full of change
And you had Kleenex
In your pockets
For your runny nose
And bleeding heart
It never bled as much as mine
Though
You were the first
And
You were the last
When will I move on?
When I hear of your death
Later on in the day
When I have nothing better to do
I will think
Think of you
And your grave
That gets no respect
From me
I never got it in life
You will never get it in death
Til do us part in death

#1340

The Good Student

Take him down hard
Like all of the other days
He was a good student
At the beginning
Then it was beaten
Out of him
He became a mediocre scared student
Fearing for his life
At recess, lunch and home time
And at the odd start of the day too
Never going to the tether balls
Because of one incident
Where one of the bullies
Fired it at him
So it hit him in the back
Of the head
Just like the fists
To his face and stomach
One day his glasses were broken
And his parents blamed him
For the expensive mishap
After the kid who broke them
Denied it to his parents
And those same parents backed him up
To the beaten kid's parents
He went inward
He drank and drugged early on
First being a happy drunk
Then a sad drunk
Then an angry drunk
Finally he quit all of that shit
He never was able to get up
Again
Because

They took him down hard
When he was young
Now older
He still waits
For his luck to change
And to able to clean
Himself from his funk
Though he always wonders
When he will be clean
When "He" turned into "Me"
All I could think about
Were two things
One was that R. L. Burnside
Died today
And the other is that
I would have made
A good student of R. L. Burnside's
But now he is dead
And I am left wondering
When I will be clean

#1341

Thank You For Nothing

I would love you
But I don't know why
I would turn it all to gold
But I never learned that
In school
So it will be years
Before I am well read
And even longer
Before I love you
And longer yet
When I turn lead
Into gold
Listen to the latest record
And it speaks to me
Like nothing before
Before I realize
I am always misunderstood
I am 13
I am born to lose
And you rub it in
If my ship comes in
I would like to thank you
Thank you then
For nothing

#1342

Guitar In Need Of Fixing

I was always out of tune
And now
I got burned up
In last year's riots
I never bowled anyone over
In school
It was always
Me feeling out of place
Hoping I would find someone
Who would help me
Not loathe me
Not loathe myself
But I never did
What confidence I had
Was a fraud
What courage I had
Was a lark
All the fires that burned
My first few pieces
Were mixed with
My peace of mind
And now
I am still out of tune

#1343

We walk through the forest
I am holding a gun in your back
We get to a secluded point
And I tell you to turn around
You hold up a large mirror
And I shoot my reflection
In the middle of my forehead
And I drop the gun
And die

#1344

Regret Is Regrettable

I always walk alone
I don't know why
I look to the buildings above
And I hope
I always hope
Someone will find me
But I know
They never will
I don't know
Where all of my friends
Have gone
And why they have gone
I sometimes feel responsible
But one shouldn't feel
Responsible
For another's ignorant actions
There will be fall out
For their ignorance
And I hope that it is radioactive
And falls on them
"You never call."
One
You changed your number
And never told me
Two
You never called me
And my number hasn't changed
In over 14 years
So what is your excuse?
Now I always walk alone
So
What is my excuse?
We went through that already

#1345

Lady Luck

She never looked my way
I am so talented
But I never got a break
My sisters on the other hand
Are in bed with her
Along with their talents
She walked out on my brother
Recently
But she is slowly coming back
In baby steps
Still
She never looks my way
And if I am so damn talented
Then why can't I make a living
Without mooching
Off of my friends?
I hope one day
She will look my way
So I can get out
Of this mess
And then I can help others
Get out of their messes

#1346

Like Lovers

Last night I dreamt
That we slept together
Like lovers
I woke up from the dream
Sad
Because I was still alone
It was 4 AM
So I made breakfast
And went to the nearest
Convenience store for a drink
I told the lady clerk
That I would see her later
She said,
"Promise, tomorrow?"
I said sure
And unless death comes my way
I won't break my promise
Unlike all of the promises
Past lovers have made to me
They were all broken
By broken lovers
To a broken boy
The boy was
And is me
I still feel like a virgin
Even though that is long gone
Last night I had a nightmare
It was that we slept together
With our backs to each other
Clutching knives in our hands
Just like lovers

#1347

Pathetic

One day
When it was windier
Than the last day
I bought a couple of
Lottery tickets
Hoping that my ship
Would come in
In one fell swoop
I always dread the day
I go to check them
Feeling foolish for wasting
Two to four dollars
On a one in fourteen million chance
It is days like this
That I regret
Not telling my Grandfather
That I loved him
Before he died
He probably knew
But after he died
I made a promise to myself
To say "I love you."
More often
To the ones
Who matter the most
Before the opportunity
Slips away
One day
When it was windier
Than the last day
I cried
Because my ship
Never came in
And I never said I love you

And when will my
Ship come in?
And even if it does
My Grandfather
Won't see it
And now I feel more
Pathetic
Than ever

#1348

Tomorrow

Tomorrow
I will win the lottery
Tomorrow
I will go on a diet
Tomorrow
I will work out
Tomorrow
I will fall in love
With a woman
Who will fall in love
With me
Tomorrow
I will not waste
So much money
Tomorrow
I will save more money
Tomorrow
I will save some money
Tomorrow
I will get published
Tomorrow
I will be more sensitive
To others
Tomorrow
I will be less sensitive
About myself
Tomorrow
I will care more
Tomorrow
My luck will change
For the better
But

Tomorrow

Never comes

#1349

The Rookie

I get around
For a rookie
I am always the rookie
Who never gets a chance
A shot
At the big time
On the eve of a new book
Spending all of my savings
On a new book
Hoping that this will work out
For the better
Not knowing
What anything ever brings
Nothing is ever sure
Except that I make mistakes
Is this new book another one?
Will I still be a rookie?
Even though I get around
"I get around"
It sometimes seems
"I get around"
About as much as
An unmailed postcard
In a lonely small town gas station
"I get around"
Shit
Do I really "get around?"

#1350

I Lie And Hide

I lie and hide
I lie about my truth from you
I hide my passions from you
Because when you spurn me
For my truths and passions
My world comes apart
At the seams
This is all for the kids
Who feel this way
And who get the same reaction
From loved ones
All your life
You were never good enough
And when you are proud
You are knocked down
By loved ones
Who subsidize other loved ones
And leave you out to rot
You tell others that
"It doesn't hurt."
But it does
And so
You lie and hide
From all around you
So you don't go to tears

And so
You lie and hide
Lie and hide

#1351

Hopefully, A Wrong Prediction

Today
I will write down
That my new book
Will be my most successful
Tomorrow
I will throw out
This page because
It won't come true

#1352

Bukowski Never Did This

I want to start a riot
So I won't have
To be an accessory
To you
Because you keep on
Stealing my ideas
And claiming them
As your own
What do you know
He is a professional writer
So he is one up on
You
And I am bleeding
All over these pages
So he is one up on
Me

I want to start a new riot
One that won't end
Until the Rolling Stones
Retire
Which, by the way,
Should have been
30 years ago
I guess Kurt Cobain and Eddie Vedder
Had a riot over 10 years ago
So now I am late again
Never on time
Even my new book was written
Almost 13 years ago
Never on time
I am always behind

I want to finish this riot

And be prepared
For a follower
To start a new one
We are all artists
To a certain degree
And eventually
We will all break through
And then riots will happen
More and more frequently
With amateur writers
Amateur painters amateur photographers
And amateur sculptors, chefs
And etc., etc., etc.
Finishing what dead old farts like
Bukowski started

#1353

Poser

Nobody knows I am paralyzed
Nobody knows I am a loser
I am dying here
And nobody knows it but me
Everybody knows I have
A shaved head, tattoos,
A pot belly, a camera
And my art
And most times
You don't see the good
And neither do I
We just meet
Once in awhile
We look in each other's eyes
And say
"I give you me,
I give you nothing."
And most times
We don't see the good
We just play the game
And then go our separate ways
Feeling that everybody knows
What is best for us
Except us

#1354

Language

You said to me
That you spoke
Another language
Well
That is cool I guess
But I created my own
Language

#1355

One Step

I glance
Every once in awhile
Over my shoulder
To see who is following me
Then I change courses
Just to keep them
As well as myself
On our toes
As well as keeping
One step ahead
Of the rest of the pack

#1356

Judas

Someday
One day
Someone close to you
Will leave you
The way you left me
And it will rip you apart
Because you won't know
Or even understand why
The same thing
The exact same thing
I went through
Several times before
With small people like you
I will pass on
And you will get nothing
Except that someone
That certain someone
Leaving you
And you won't be able to ask
Even their shadow
Why?

#1357

Ground Beef And Pineapple Pizza

During high school
And a little while after
Graduation
We were the best friends
Eating
Ground beef and pineapple pizza
And drinking lots of beer
At a little Italian place upstairs
From the coin and card shop
On Whyte Avenue in Edmonton
It was never busy there
So we had a blast
By ourselves
Just being teenagers
Making fun of each other
Making fun of everyone else
And you said that you were angry
That your former best friend
Ditched you because
He got a girlfriend
This was over several
Pitchers of beer
And lots of pizza
I thought of this all
As I ate my
Ground beef and pineapple pizza
By myself today
The taste and smell
Brought it all back
And how about a year after
You said this to me
You got a girlfriend
And became a born again christian
To this very day

I have not heard from you
Maybe it worked out for the better
I don't drink alcohol anymore
And I am anti-religion
So now all I've got
Is my fading memories
About beer and you
While I eat my
Ground beef and pineapple pizza
By myself
Alone in my small apartment
With my bitterness and loneliness
And some sadness
About my fading memories
About another former "best friend"

#1358

Fix My Head

The other day
The sound
That came from my head
Was deafening
I know what's going on
Enough
To know what's going on
No
I don't believe in you
Because
You are a pot smoking drunk
And I am in a self made prison
And your chance of changing
Is about as high
As me fixing my head
So I listen to more Black Flag
And pass out in my bed
Disturbed
By the day's goings ons
Because I have got nothing
Better to do
When the shit hits the fan
And I collapse
At your feet
Every time I call you
I know
I know
I know
Punk rules
Okay
OK
OK
OK
So I stumble along

And hope that I get it right
This time
I know
I am always wanting more
So
You are too
But smoking so much dope
Doesn't help your asthma
And me dwelling on the negative
Doesn't help me with
This
The other day
When I realized
I have a certain loyalty
To this prison
Because that is where
I
Became who
I am
Today

#1359

Let's Talk

I climbed a ladder
To the clouds
And forgot all
That was below
And wasted no time
In finding a new place
To hide
From the memories
Of below
Because the past
Always haunts me
And when I found a way
To escape it
I took it
Hook
Line
And sinker
And
That
Ended
Everything
Below
Held
For
Me
Now I hope that the clouds
Are full of hope and desire
So that
I will never need to sleep
Again

#1360

"No man is an island."
Fuck you
Every man is an island bitch cakes
I didn't think it was funny
Not one bit
But everyone laughed anyways
And you wonder why
I feel like an island?

#1361

Elliott

I listened to your record today
And I wondered
What it felt like
To be a bride's maid
To an "Oscar" win
And then I wondered
What it felt like
To plunge your knife
Deep into your chest
Until your own life slipped away

I feel like
Plunging a knife
Deep into my chest
To take my own life
Every time my shrink
Asks me if I want to
Kill anyone
"It is my job." he says
But I know that he doesn't trust me
And yet I am supposed
To trust him with my life

He doesn't get it
And I am supposed to be happy
One day before my 34th birthday
On this Remembrance Day
When my writer friends
Write that November
Is the most depressing month
Of the year
They don't get it
But I have to ask myself
On this Remembrance Day

Do I even get it?

this piece was written
on November 11, 2005
in Edmonton

#1362

Strange days like these
Have an impact on me
So that I hide out
And listen to too much
Nick Drake and Elliott Smith
I am so frail
Because my emotional army
Has surrendered
To the grey skies outside

#1363

Four

I break my heart
Everyday
By thinking of you
Everyday

I amputate my legs
So I can't run back
To you or
Run away from your memory

I read to small crowds
So that the large crowds
Won't lynch me and
The small crowds forget about me

I am a broken hearted amputee
With haunting memories
That the small crowds love
And the large crowds ignore

#1364

At night
I wander around and around
On the avenue of fools
(Me being one of the fools
For wandering around on the avenue)
Not sure where I am going
Over and over
Again
Without you
But at least I have myself
Somewhere
In between
My apartment's silence
And the noise of
The avenue of fools
At night

#1365

It Isn't My Fault

It isn't my fault
Things went wrong
And it isn't my fault
That everything is going right
It isn't my fault
That you fell through the cracks
And I was put on a pedestal
It isn't my fault
That I am <u>not</u> a revolutionary
And I am the one Roman candle
Lit in the center
Of a football field
On a dark Wednesday night

I am not sure
If it is my fault
They don't call me anymore
I am not sure
If it is my fault
I will never know about their baby
If I am your friend
Don't stop returning my calls
Do tell me what I did wrong
And I will try with all of my power
To fix it
I want to be your friend too
But I am not sure

If this is
Or isn't
My fault

#1366

Along The Way

It is a long road
Waiting for you to call
Always hoping I don't get lost
Along the way
Meanwhile
I woke up from a dream
About the three guys
In RUN DMC
And how they came back to Edmonton
And were as popular as
Posers like "50 cent"
This would have been the second time
That I saw them
And instead of praising
Addidas shoes
And god
And clean living
They were feeding the crowd
At the stadium
Shitty food and
Loads of alcohol
I bragged to some black kid
How the last time I saw them
Was years ago and
They were playing
In a shitty little bar called "Cowboys"
And that 95% of the crowd was white
And now it was vice verso
And the kid was in awe
And I was eating the shitty food
And drinking lots of beer
Not thinking once that
Hey!
I don't drink alcohol

Or eat shitty food
Like that anymore!
And I realized
That in my dream
I had sold out
Just as much as
RUN DMC had sold out
In my dream
And I prayed that
You would call
To wake me from this nightmare
But the phone was as silent
As a crypt
The same sort of crypt that
Jam Master Jay rested in now
Or as silent as my room in this case
When I woke
From this play gone wrong
I realized that no one could save me
From my nightmares
I was doomed
To being an overweight,
Alcoholic, drug addict
And as for RUN DMC
They all died
When I woke up
And so did I
Because I got lost
Along the way

#1367

Bad Luck

A short while ago
A woman made fun of me
For not having sex
For 9 years
My comeback was
To tell her that it would be
Another 9 years
Or maybe more
Because I wasn't
In love with her
So, naturally, I wasn't going
To have sex with her

That was what
The few women
I had sex with
Had in common
I was in love with them
That is my basis
For having sex with a woman
To at the very least, like her alot
Or, preferably, love her
And preferably it would be mutual

As for the woman
Who made fun of me
She spit in my face
Said I probably had a small dick
And that I should
Go fuck myself
And then she left
I haven't seen her since

I then realized that

I have a way with women
And that it probably
Would be another 9 years or so
Before I had sex with one
Because of my way with women

#1368

About You

I dreamt of being with you last night
I couldn't help it
The dream was more
Than I wanted to see
But I couldn't help it
Because I had been thinking
About you
All the previous day
I told you
I couldn't help it
Because the heat
In my apartment
Was stifling
And there you were
In my head
All polished and pretty
And there I was
In my bed
All fat and covered in tattoos
And just ripe for a nice dream
For once
I am truly sorry
I couldn't help it
I promise you
It won't happen again
Because the river
Was black and churning violently
And I thought that it would take
All of my bad dreams and
Good ones too
Away
Far away
Far far away
I dreamt of pulling off

A daring bank heist
I dreamt of not pissing
On the edge of the bowl
I dreamt of executing the death penalty
On a child molester
I dreamt of not being late
For work
I dreamt of being a positive
Role model and/or icon for youth
I dreamt of not leaving stains
In my underwear
And I dreamt of being with you
So
If I took a picture
Of a dream I just had
Would you tell me what you saw?
Or not even look?
Just telling me
I am just a fad
Or would you look
And then slap me in the face
And tell me to get over it
And to grow up
And do it
Right now
Because right now
I feel guilty as
A catholic murderer
With a conscience
In confession
You can't describe
The way I feel
When I can barely
Do it myself
And all of these dreams
Haunt me through the day
Because they almost always
Never come true

#1369

The Winners And Losers

All the moments
That we could share
Go out the window
When your boyfriend asks me
If I drink
I tell him "no"
And leave early and quickly
I don't think you know
That I think about you
All of the time
All of my down time
All of the moments
That we could share
Are flushed away
When I hear you
Call me "friend"
And I finally know
Who's the winner
And who's the loser

#1370

Helping You Move

I painted over the walls
That we made love against
And now you're long gone
And I am moving out too
I also left all of the lights on
When I went to bed
The same bed that we slept together in
And now you're long gone
And I am moving out too
In the new year
With all of my art, books and records
Of what little we accomplished
Together
We were broken when we came together
Now we are broken when we broke up
Do you get this?
No
You are long gone
And I am always moving out too

#1371

Fools On The Avenue: Part 2

I saw a drunk kid
With urine soaked pants
Crouching
And taking a shit
A few feet from the sidewalk
I saw graffiti on a seat
At a bus stop that said
Drinking
Fucking
Fighting
Beer
If everything dies
I hope you all die
Sooner than later
Go home and fuck off
Not in that order
Now you can't smoke
In all of the bars
So I saw a group of young men
Smoking outside a bar
And one of them
Was pissing on the sidewalk
Around here there is just
Winners and losers
And you shitheads
Make me feel like
I am on the wrong side
When it is you
Who are the losers
When all you find worthwhile
In life is
Drinking
Fucking
Fighting

And beer
I hope for the cold to come
And freeze you all to death
Or I hope for the rain to come
And wash and drown you all away
And somehow clean up this mess
Once and for all

#1372

Fools On The Avenue: Part 3

I will be a rebel
Tonight
By going to bed
Without brushing my teeth
On the way home
Some asshole
On the phone
Asked me
If I could
Spare some change
I told her that I had no money
(Which was true)
She told me to have
A happy new year
It was snowing
Just like the last time
I saw DJ Joy alive
I took photos of one of his raves
And called him
After I processed them
He never returned my first 2 phone calls
And on the third phone call
The phone number was disconnected
I figured
Just another person
Who blew me off
Until
I get a call a couple of months later
From his girlfriend
Telling me that he was killed
In a hit and run
They still don't know who did it
This was several years ago
And now

I see people fighting
I see people puking
I hear people getting drunk
Listening to shitty top 40 music
Right now I am listening to
"Soul Jacker" by Eels
And I think of how
I never have fun
On new year's eve anymore
He said
If you are afraid of dying
Then you had better not be afraid of living
I wish it would freeze
I wish A.I.D.S. would selectively kill
The dumb drunks I see every night
On my way home
I am just tired
I am just tired
I am just tired
Tired of the fools on the Whyte Avenue
Happy new year
Assholes
Happy new year

        this piece was written at 11:39 PM
            on December 31, 2005
                in Edmonton

#1373

Not Soon Enough

You come into my life
Like a spring breeze
But smelling of cigarettes
And alcohol
Telling me of how
You are going to therapy now
When we embrace
I tell you that
I like how you feel
You say the same
But I am never quite sure
If you would rather
I wasn't 80 pounds overweight
I tell you that
I miss you
And that you should call me
Sometime
But I know you never will
And you never do
Spring breeze
Changes into fall chill
And I am left alone
Again
Wondering
Again
When spring will come
Because it can't come
Soon enough

#1374

Going Into The City

Going into the city
The bus ride to the record store
Was almost 45 minutes
It was worth it
I am currently listening
To the Clash's first record
It reminds me of
Going into the city
To go to the record store
And getting some of my fix
My saviour
My only true friend
In junior high school
And high school
I would drop almost all
Of my paper route money
Every second weekend
This was all done against
My parent's wishes
They both thought it was a
Waste of money
They just didn't realize
That it was the opposite
My fix
My saviour
My only true friend
R.E.M., Clash, Fugazi, The Cure, Misfits, Circle Jerks, Nomeansno, S.N.F.U., Dead Kennedys, Soundgarden, The Alarm, U2, 7 Seconds, D.O.A., Metallica, Iggy Pop, Crass, Subhumans, Sonic Youth, Soul Asylum, Neil Young, Bob Dylan, Joni Mitchell, Midnight Oil, Husker Du, Black Flag, Black Sabbath, Conflict, Big Black
And the list goes on and on and on...

I still collect music
To be my fix
To be my savior
To be my only true friend
But it is different now
Somewhere along the way
I discovered myself
In all those scratchy records
And I started
To write
To paint
To take photographs
And in these
Forms of expression
I found
Another fix
Another saviour
Another true friend
This got me through
The 90's and 2000's
The music got me through
The 80's and 90's
When I picked up
My pen
My brush
My camera
I don't recall
Burning any bridges
Because all of the old and new
Music is still my fix
Music is still my saviour
And my true friend

#1375

A New Car

Looking in my rear view
Wondering when I will look
Through the front window instead
Possibly seeing the future
Maybe it won't be as bleak
As the rear view
Maybe it won't be as desperate
As what sits next to me
An empty seat
Maybe it will all work out
If I hang in there
Maybe

#1376

Letters To A Writer

I went out for a walk
This morning
I dodged the cigarette butts
And vomit and dog shit
I talked with a lady
I have got along with
At the 7-11
She has been a manager
For a couple of years
And is slowly getting tired
Of her work
Of her staff
Who act like babies
Most of the time
Most of the time
She gets by
But today she seemed tired
So I buy a lottery ticket
And tell her that it is our
Retirement plan
I get home and talk
With my ailing Grandmother
Who lives in central Manitoba
It is about a 12 hour car ride
From here to there
Why are you laughing?
Did I make a joke?
I am always out of sync
With everyone else around me
People often stop
Calling me
And/or
Returning my calls
Imagine going from

Total obscurity to
Even more total obscurity
I used to want to leave a mark
In this world
But now I just want to vanish
On a walk
Near my ailing Grandmother's farm

#1377

When I told you
No offense
I meant it
No
Offense
I am more creative than you
That is the truth
There is no need
To cry yourself to sleep
Cheer up
Because the truth
Sometimes hurts
Cheer up
I hope that you can

#1378

Empty Pockets At An Arm's Length

No matter what you do
No matter who you do
We never catch up
You disappear
With my phone number
Never to make that call
When I need it most
You never turn to me
Because I never had
A pocket full of gold
Or silver
I just get by
Yes
Maybe that's it
Maybe you want more
Than I can give
You
No matter what I do
No matter who you do
I am always at an arm's length
To you

#1379

This Time

Fractured words and bones
In a hotel on the avenue
Just as bad
As giving up
After 35 years
Of good service
Move on
Move along
Keep moving
Nothing to see here
Nothing to hear
From nothing to hearing
From nothing to here
From nowhere to here
At last
These fractured words and bones
Have a home
Where one never wins
But where one is always working hard
At working hard
In a hotel on the avenue
Where people waste their time
Every weekend
Move on
Move along
Keep moving
Moving on up
From nowhere to there this time
This time
I will get it right
This time
I will miss you
Because you said it aloud
And I just thought it quietly

At last
Alas
I just thought it quietly
I just thought this all quietly
To myself
And moved along
Shuffling out of your way
Back to my home
Where no one ever wins

#1380

It Is About Respect

I need no alibi
Honestly
This is going to get preachy
Fuck Valentine's day
Fuck Christmas
Fuck New Year's day
Fuck Mother's day
Fuck Father's day
Fuck Grandparent's day
And fuck your birthday
All of these are just
Corporate circle jerks
If you only show respect
To your family, lover and friends
On these select few days
Then you are a shithead
Who should be dismembered
And fed to the wolves
What about August fourth?
Don't recognize that one?
That's because it hasn't been
Designated yet dumb ass
Same with March 29th
What about November eleventh?
All the stores are open that day
My Grandfather was in
World War 2 and Korea
And all you pricks worry
About him and other veterans
One day out of the year
What about the other days
Of the year?
Including the corporate ass grab ones?
It is about respect

If you can't show your love
Of your lover
Every day of the year
Then you shouldn't have a lover
And that goes for all the other
Corporate holidays
It is about respect
Show love and respect
To your loved ones
On a regular basis
And you will see it come back to you
Twice fold
Merry Christmas?!
Fuck off!
Random acts of kindness week?!
Fuck that you tool!
Do random acts of kindness
Every day
And maybe
Just maybe
The world wouldn't be so full of
Hate and bigotry and such
Honestly
I need no alibi
I just hope that you have a good day

>   this piece was written at 3:40 PM
>   on February 15, 2006
>   in Edmonton

#1381

Disguising My Tears

It is only rain
So it is your money
Or your life
And right now
While it is pissing down
It would take too much energy
For your life
So just give me your money
And I will let you go
Without a scar
Even though
You left me years ago
With a nasty scar
So I would rather have money
Than fame
This is one direct quote
Get that?
One direct quote
So it is only rain
And it is disguising my tears
That make my scar worse
So thanks for the money
See you next week

#1382

Confrontational

Late at night
Is when
It is the worst
The loneliness hits me
Like a sledgehammer
I have no one to blame
But myself
Or at least
That's how the small people
Make me feel
I got a note from
A friend from high school
And he says
We haven't talked
In several years
And he doesn't know why
I remember
Giving him my phone number
Three times
And my number hasn't changed
In 15 years
And his was disconnected
3 months after I last talked
To him
How many times do I have to
Give my number out to the same person
How many times do I have to
Bang my head against that brick wall
So I was the nice guy
And gave him my number
A fourth time
He is not a small person though
The small people
Are the ones who

Give you their number
And you talk a few times
And then they never return
Your calls
Now I know what my bald head is for
Banging it against that brick wall
Now I know what my hairy balls are for
Being kicked in every other week
Now I know what my sharp pen is for
Passing the time
Late at night

#1383

I don't think you would
Have done it this way
But I am doing it
This way
And I don't mind it
One bit

So why should you?

#1384

How Do I Start?

I have a crush
On a belly dancer
I almost had it
The last time we talked
But I couldn't pull the trigger
So I'll wait
A little while longer
With all of the doubts
Of an alcoholic angel
I have seen an angel
And I reacted
Like she was the devil
Because the way
That she moves
Temporarily blinds my eyes
And I was so gripped by fear
That I walked away
When a voice inside me
Told me
To go for it
I am tired of
Just getting by
I am tired of
Just surviving
I want to excel
And be the bomb
In her life
And be the light
At the end of the tunnel
In mine
Because
I believe
That's how it should be
In affairs of the heart

#1385

Worse Than The Last Time

On my way home
From work one Friday night
I ran into her
I hadn't seen her in about a year
She used to be a junkie alcoholic
Now she is just an alcoholic
She put me on the guest list
With her to see a couple of bands
At a nearby bar
Even though she forgot my name
She told me of her
Latest line of problems
She was arrested
For selling pills to a cop
And plead guilty
So she wouldn't do time
Now she has a curfew of 11 PM
And it was well past 11 PM
When she told me that
She was 93 pounds
And the same height as me
And had cancer
And had a daughter
Ten years going on twenty she said
She was a little drunk
And I had to go
To catch the last bus
I wished her well
She said thanks
And that someone
Would look after her
When I left
I wondered who
Because her husband

Was at home with leukemia

The band I saw was great
But they didn't ease my feeling
Of helplessness around her
All the way home
I wondered if that would be
The last time I ever see her alive

#1386

System

It is not a drill
It is not a test
Of the emergency broadcast system
It is the real thing
And I am always told
I am stepping on someone else's
Toes
Then for a few years
I say to myself
Never again
Never again
At least she was honest
With my twisted psychology
At least I didn't do it
Face to face
At least
At least
At least
It is always at least
It is never the most
It is just a drill
It is just a test
Of the emergency broadcast system
It is never the real thing
Never again.

Never again?

#1387

Trust No One

She was on a high
For the rest of the day
I was on a low
For the rest of the year
So I learned
Never to open up to anyone
Because she was flattered
But flattery got me nowhere
It was such a waste
Fighting with myself
For days on end
Only to hear
No.
This one is for me
No one else
Because the mistakes I make
Feel like anvils on my shoulders
So this one is for me
Because something inside
Always dies
When I hear
No.
No more
I won't give out
Any more
You will have to pay
To get it out of me
It is always a big deal
For me
But never for them
I bought a ticket
And my boat came in
And just missed my dock
By about 100 yards

So I went home
Ate
Tried to sleep
But tossed restlessly
It used to be special
But now it is just like
Those one dollar
Mass produced toys from China
That sit on shelves
Gaining dust
In an old dollar store
What if Maurice Richard
Quit after his third injury?
It was never asked
Or was an issue
Because he was just getting on a roll
And now
He is a hero to many
And I am still hearing
No.
And never getting on a roll
I don't know quite how to say it
More clearly than this

Trust no one

#1388

Glad To Meet You

Follow me down
To some kind of party
Where we both get along
Where all of the shit
From the past is forgotten
And we move on
Where there is life
Outside of work
Outside of our homes
Outside of our flesh
The division has been made
You won't follow me
And now I made
The same mistake twice
I will never learn?
Will I never learn?
Will I ever learn?
When will I learn?

#1389

At The End Of The Day

There must be a better way
There must be a cleaner way
To get by
Without getting hurt so bad
All of the time
This onslaught must end
Onslaught of bad luck
Bad timing
Ill will
And blind eyes
That only see
When it is convenient
Suppose I was only to write
About happiness
Nature
Love
Would you see me then?
How must I change
Before you accept me?
There must be a better way
Before you get involved
With me
At the end of the day

#1390

Letter To My Brother

This is the best gift
I could think of
For your 38th birthday
You came into my life
Almost 10 years ago
And everything is sweeter now
You and your wife
Are vegans who
Catch and release
Bees that burrow
Into your home
And carpenter ants
That eat your home
I tried calling you today
Several times
And each time
The line was busy
I just thought
I would let you know
That I may not agree
With your catch and release program
And I like ice cream
But I have respect for you
Sticking to your guns
This may embarrass you but
Happy birthday
With love
Corey

#1391

Names:Part 2

Listening to Chan Marshall
Weep
Through my stereo all day
Put me through the ringer
And made me think
About all of the friends
I have lost
Murray in elementary school
Sean and his sister in junior high school
Mike 2 years ago
Jigger about 4 years now
There is more
But I don't want to hear it
I just want to hear
Ms. Marshall
With her beautiful voice
With her guitar
With her piano
Struggling to get through
A song called "Names"
She doesn't know
Where they all went
The people I named
I just know that they
Aren't suffering anymore
Most people I know
I pushed away
And never heard from again
I hope that they
Never end up
In a poem
Like this

#1392

Happy Easter

We all drove 12 hours
To Manitoba to see my Grandmother
Mary Hamilton
My Dad's mom
She was ecstatic to see us all
My Mom, Dad and I
Drove in one van
While my 2 younger sisters
And their respective husbands
Drove in one car
The Sunday we had a wiener roast
It was a beautiful sunny day plus 25 degrees
On my Grandmother's farm
The farm had been in the Hamilton family
For one hundred years this year
I am sitting next to my Grandma
We had just finished a conversation
When her smiling face
Went limp and blank
And then she buckled over
In her brand new walker
Her Puerto Viarta hat
Her daughter (my Aunt) had bought for her
Tumbled to the ground
Along with her co-op diet lemon lime soda
Falling on her leg
Then on my leg
Then to the ground
I stood up and looked to my Dad
And I almost barked
(Sorry Dad)
"Get a cell phone and call 911."
My youngest sister hands him her phone
I turned around to see

My youngest sister's husband
Removing her teeth
(He works in the medical field)
And saying over and over again
"Mrs. Hamilton, Mrs. Hamilton..."
She was not responding
I heard my Dad say into the phone
"Rossburn
Ron Hamilton's farm
1 mile east
2 miles south"
Twenty seconds felt like an eternity but
Finally
My Grandma opened her eyes slightly
My brother in law asked,
"What would you like Mrs. Hamilton?"
She responded weakly
"I...want...my teeth."
She just fainted

We wrapped up
And Grandma said sadly
"I ruined the party."
We tried to reassure her that
Everything was OK
And that we were wrapping up anyways
I thought to myself
That by dodging the death card again
She made the Easter long weekend
The happiest I have had in a long time
Thanks Grandma
For still being there
Love Corey

#1393

I Shouldn't Have Said It

I regret saying
"I love you."
To you
I regret not saying
"I forgot your name."
To you
That was the last time
I saw you
I don't know where you are
And that is OK
From now on
It will rain forever
Until I forgive you
And until I forgive myself

#1394

These Memories

These memories
Will never be forgotten
Your words are like
My scars from myself
And the surgeon
Who inspected me
This comes from the future
To haunt your past
And to make sure that your present
Is decimated
To the point of no return
So even if I don't show
My face
In your place anymore
You will know why

It is because
These memories
Will never be forgotten

#1395

Life Of Longing

When I hear people prefer
Hockey to Judo
It is solitude
When I hear people prefer
Union dues to working hard
It is solitude
You know that I will be around
I may be late
But I will always be around
I am a little boy
Carrying a pail of water
In a desert
And I should have
Drank the water
Months ago
Oh you're a sweet thing
But you don't know it
Oh I am so miserable
With my feet in the air
And my back in the grass
You can take a hint
But you still can't let go
I long to be with you
But I am old enough
To be your father
I have held you in my arms
I have kissed you on the lips
But all I can think about
Is the daughter I never had
And when you will actually call me
And you know
I will always be around

#1396

Right's Right Rights

He's going off to war
With me in the back seat
Whether I like it or not
I really believe
That
What goes around
Comes around
And all of the references
You distort
Will come back to haunt you
He worked for a platform
And he's entitled to use it
Let's not impeach him
Let's do what they did
To Mussolini
To him
You live in the shadows
Of your religion
And breaking every law
Not for love
But for hate
I have no rights anymore
So I have become
An American at war

New Project

I am still waiting
For you to call me
I am still foolishly waiting
For you to call me
I know I can breathe
Without you
But it is catching me
When I am vulnerable
That gets to me
I know when I see you next
It will be excuses and/or lies
And I will be embarrassed
And want to die
I am still foolishly waiting
For one of your kind
To bring me a heaven
I have made up my own
But now it is the time
For one more
No more roller coaster
Just sunflowers for the eyes
And their smell for the nose
And their seeds for the mouth
And
And
And
I am still waiting

#1398

And With Myself

Listening to the history
Of Joy Division and Ian Curtis
On a beat up radio
And it gets me all sad
And wanting
And longing
And even needing
A change
I need it
Something has to go right
For once
I need it
Eat the little food I have
And take my meds
And hope that someone
Comes calling for my work
10:48 AM on a Sunday morning
Thinking about
The Carla Bozulich/Silver Mount Zion show
And how I met
Carla Bozulich
And how she forgot about me
Minutes after I left
And how that is how
It always goes
I feel like I am slowly killing myself
With loneliness
And always being tired
I want my ashes
Scattered over the valley
Near my Grandfather Hamilton's grave
To make piece
With him
And with myself

I am tired of all the
Drinking and smoking you do
And I am tired of all the
Eating and listening I do
The vision is blurred
To make it a safer view
Listening to history
And taking my meds
With loneliness
And with myself
Knowing full well
That Ian was right
Love <u>will</u> tear us apart

#1399

So Long

So long
Not so hopeful
Not so positive
Waiting for you
Knowing that you are
Just 10 blocks away
And you always say
That you'll call me
But you never do
I need it
I need it
I have seen you in the flesh
I have held you in my arms
And kissed you on the lips
And that's where it ended
A silent phone
Not so hopeful
Not so positive
Waiting for you
So long

#1400

Here I Am Again

It's the way you act
On the outside
That contradicts
The way you feel
On the inside
I don't feel for you
I feel nothing for you
When you hang up on me
In public
For the hundredth time
There can be no
Passing the buck
For the hundredth time
Friend
Is not in my vocabulary
When I think of you
Fold this up
Into a small square
And pass it around
All of your circle of friends
And they will all walk
Away
With wonder and amazement
At how I keep
Falling into your arms
Falling into your lips
Falling into your shallow chasm
Of hollow promises
You used to be the only one
Then I went away
For the hundredth time
And it was
Out of sight
Out of mind

Out of touch
For the hundredth time
And now I dread
Your sight
Your smell
Your touch
Your words
And
Your
Acts
Of lack of discipline
And
Now
My disciplines
Won't let me live
Without a memory of you
And a fear
Of seeing you
And hearing your
False promises
For the hundredth time

It's the way you feel
On the outside
That contradicts
The way you act
On the inside
For the hundredth time

#1401

Nice Little Packages

She is allergic to my art
But not me
She is allergic to me
But not my art
I am not convenient
Or in a mall
Like their shit
Life is sailing by
All three of us
But she dropped me
Like a hot potato without remorse
And the other dropped me
Like an apple with all of the regret
In the world
Although
You never can be sure
With the two of them
Because they were never
Runaways
And I am always
Running away from something
Never able to catch my breath
And always looking behind me

#1402

Last Night

After waking
From strange sexual dreams
I am left sweaty
And uncomfortable
About going back to sleep
It became routine last night
It happened 3 or 4 times
So now I sit in my underwear
And scars
Tired and worn out
Wanting sleep more now
Than ever before
I am tired
And I am listening to Cat Power
Again
I am tired
Again
And everybody is not around
Again
And I am one now
Again
Without everybody
And
I think that
I am brave enough now
That I am one
Again
And I think that
I will try and sleep
Again

#1403

Rural In The Urban

I like finding
The rural in the urban
Weeds on unused railway tracks
Old broken down cars in alleys
Old houses on an old tree lined street
It all makes me feel like
I am in the town
Where my Grandmother Hamilton lives
I treasure these moments
Caught in time
And it all makes me sleep easier
With pleasant dreams

#1404

I Hate Buses

I always feel
I am getting vertigo
On buses
The loud noises
The loud smells
The loud sights
Drunks, gangster wannabes,
Girls who always talk
Loud on cell phones
And girls who always talk
Loud
I hate buses

#1405

Whose Were These?

Whose shoes
Were these?
A drunk's?
A frat boy's?
A dead person's?
Or were they so worn out
That the former owner
Just tossed them away
And moved on?
In socks?
In bare feet?
In someone else's shoes?
Or new ones
He bought at the local
Army & Navy?
Whose shoes
Were these?

#1406

Night Time On The Avenue

The fools on the avenue
Constantly asking me what I am doing
Telling me to take pictures of them
Drunks staring
While they take a piss on the avenue
People running red lights
All captured on film
I would like to send the avenue
Business Association and Foundation
Copies of photos
Of losers taking crap on the train tracks
Of losers bleeding and puking on the sidewalk
Of all the cigarette butts and trash
And in my letter it would say,
"You created this mess.

#1407

Respect For The 7-11 Workers

Respect
That is what I have
For all of the workers at the
24 hour store
For putting up with the thieves
The drunks
The junkies
The rude lottery ticket buyers
And the rude people in general

I hope that you 7-11 workers get out in time
Before you end up bitter like me

Warning

Slow down please
Children are playing
Signs warning you
Of children playing
Children are so innocent
They don't think that
They will ever get hurt
But then adults
Come along
And distort or corrupt
Everything
Be careful with the children
They are fragile

#1409

Nothing Like The Clouds

Clouds
Any kind
Stormy ones
Fluffy white ones
Or even the occasional haze
I could stare at clouds
In the sky for hours
Even the black foreboding storm clouds
I find peace in
Even if it just brings rain
And a light and sound show
Clouds
Any kind
Put me at ease

#1410

Contrast

The white on red
The black on white
The red on blue
The green on beige
And finally the stone on foliage
Especially the soft fluffy kind
That makes graffiti covered stone
Look harder than it is

Contrast in life
I believe are beautiful
Even if it is an ugly contrast
By today's standards
It is still wonderful
Unintentional intentional
I believe contrast and
Contrasts make the world go around

Love For Flowers

I am a man
Who likes to get flowers
From women I like
I am a man
Who likes to give flowers
To women I like
I have only received flowers
Once in my life from a woman that I liked
But I have stopped giving flowers
To women I like
Because it usually went
Unappreciated
Luckily
This all has not tarnished
My love for flowers

#4112

Zombies In The Mall

I HATE MALLS
And all of the people
Who wander without a purpose
For hours on end
I can't stand people
Who walk slow
And hold me up from my purpose
Of finding what I need
It is like herding cattle or something
This was the only time
I was in a mall all this year
And probably the last time too

#1413

Zombies On The Avenue

I HATE CROWDS
So I go out early
To avoid the crowds
And do my business
Where I need to go
It is almost as bad
As the malls
The crowds
The people who stop
Without warning
Who cut you off
And then walk
Slower than you
Who beg for change
Who
Who
Who am I
In this crowd?
Am I just another zombie?

#1414

Bruce Lee

Bruce Lee said
Be like water
Or something of the sort
Water takes on any shape
And when it is in nature
It makes it even more special
Streams
Lakes
Marshes
The oceans
They are all special
Water takes on any shape
Whether it is warm or cold
Whether it is boiling or frozen
Water cleans the outside
Of the body
As well as the inside
Nature at its best

#1415

Architecture Is Quiet

I like making architecture
Quiet with my camera
Even the noisiest
I can make quiet
With the right angle
Good architecture is beautiful
Almost as good as nature
Well
Not really
But it is still beautifully quiet
In its own way

#1418

This Old Van

This old van
Used to be all white
Then some rocket scientist
Painted blue words
"Advertising"
On it
And made it an eye sore
I now wish I could remember it
Without the words
All over it
Sometimes
Less is better
K.I.S.S.
Keep It Simple Stupid

#1417

Lockdown Remains

Lockdown remains
A bunch of unused bicycles
A carriage
A holding container...containing what?
All locked up
Behind a chain link fence
With barbed wire on top
I feel like cutting
The fence open
And giving all of the bikes
To needy children
I don't care about
The carriage and container
But the bikes locked up
For some reason
Make me sad

#1418

Shade

I love shade
In the summer time
It is such a refuge
From the sometimes harsh sunlight
I saw a movie once
And the female main character's
Name was "Shade"
And she was the sweetest
Kindest person
In the whole movie
Ever since that movie
Shade makes me think of
The tree in my Grandmother Hamilton's old yard
And the beautiful girl in that movie is why
If I ever have children
And a girl is born
I would like to name her
Shade

#1419

Sun Down

Sunsets
Are almost as calming
As sunrises
Sunsets
Make me think of
Putting an end to a bad day
And they mean a new day
Is around the corner
And that means
A sunset is around the corner to
Start a new day off right
Sunset
Sunsets
A good day is around the corner

#1420

Most Birds

Most birds I like
Eagles to swallows
Ravens to robins
Owls to blue jays
Etc., etc., etc.
But pigeons
Seagulls and magpies
I call them all
Flying rats
To me they are pests

But on this day
A pigeon posed for me
Around some flowers
And my opinion changed
Just slightly
For one brief moment

#1421

The Weathering Process

This is not a drill
It is the real thing
Painting over
An already painted over
Guard rail
That the weather
Has already taken its toll on
If they wanted a new colour on it
Then why didn't they
Clean it all off and
Do it properly the first time?
And then the second time too?
The only good thing about it
I have more fodder for my camera and pen
Thanks.

#1422

George

I don't know his last name
But I have seen him on the avenue
Ever since I moved here
On Canada Day 1990
He moved to this part of the city
On Canada Day 1964
I don't know much about him
What I do know is
He is Polish and was in Auschwitz
He was a janitor at the law courts
He likes Second Cup coffee
And he is always the happiest man
On the avenue
This blurry photo of him smiling
Doesn't do him justice
Because when he is gone
I will miss him and his loud
"Good morning!" or "Lovely!"
I wish that he could live forever
But I know that he won't
And when he goes
I hope that his funeral is
filled with
Everyone he has touched

Sometime between the fall of 2007 and the spring of 2008 George passed away... R.I.P. George, R.I.P....

#1423

I am NOT With The Band

Lights! Camera! Action!
Loud music with lots of energy
Is the best
You can always find me
Taking pictures of bands
I have been doing it since 1988
And I rarely get paid
But usually when I do get paid
The bands appreciate my work
And sometimes
If I am lucky
I will see my work in a CD sleeve
I take pictures because
I don't want to forget
Anymore bands I see
Or saw
Or will see
Momentos of my past
And hopefully
Opportunities in the future

#1424

Solace

Solace
From the heat
Solace
From the cold
Solace
From the rain or snow
And solace
From the fools on the avenue
That is how I see Blackbyrd Myoozik
Besides that
It is a heck of a place
And the best place to find music
On the avenue

To Arthur Fafard & crew.

#1425

The Mom & Pop Store

There are not many left
Or so it seems
Of the Mom and Pop store
The place where nepotism runs rampant
And if you are lucky
And you work there
You may get paid under the table
But that is if you are lucky
Even crowded
These stores give me peace of mind
And a calm reassurance
That they will always be there
When you need them the most

#1426

Wealth

When I first went into Sound Connection
When I was about 14 or so
I was floored at all the records I saw
To this day most of my records
Have come from their wealth

One day I went into "The Marquee"
And some bleach blonde guy
Was a snob to me for buying
A Circle Jerks record
You can see this tool in
The Tragically Hip video for
"The Last American Exit"
Anyways, I never went back

Instead I felt guilty about
Betraying Sound Connection
And that same day
I went into Sound connection
And bought 12 records
The biggest haul I ever made in one store

To Dorne Hootz and his Mother, Donna Mitchel.

#1427

Dorky

That is what the current owner
Told me to call this one
When I was 16
After leaving the Marquee disappointed
And Sound Connection with a haul
I thought that I would try Freecloud
Some old guy was behind the counter
Playing folk music!
I was into punk rawk!
So I left in a huff

Things have changed in 20 years
And even if the current owner
Wants me to call this dorky
It has turned into a fine place
For record geeks like me
To haunt

To Rich Liukko & crew.

#1428

Limp Handshake

Time and time and time again
You tell me she's your girlfriend
And you fuck her
In a friend's bathroom
While other people
Drink other people's wine
Two things you are <u>not</u> supposed
To do at a friend's place
I am so tired
Of your
Time and time and time again
And of your
Smoking and drinking
And your writing
And your plagiarism
And your
Your
Your
Limp handshakes
I look forward to the day
You lose everything you own
In a tragic house fire

#1429

I get my beat
From the back of my head
Somewhere around the place
Where I think about you
All of the time

#1430

White Trash Bohemian

Oh you are so Bohemian
Because you smoke lots of dope
Oh you are so Bohemian
Because you drink other people's wine
Oh you are so Bohemian
Because you talk about how much sex you have
Oh you are so Bohemian
With that stupid fucking black beret
Oh you think you are so Bohemian
When you are really just white trash
One step away from being a dirty hippy
In fancy clothes

#1431

And Your And My

Every piece I have written
Is about you
And your hair
And your eyes
And your breasts
And your arms
And your hands
And your breath

Every piece I have yet to write
Is about me
And my medications
And my pot belly
And my tattoos
And my art
And my collection of other people's art
And my suicide

#1432

It Gets Boring

Your boyfriend
Can't handle his liquor
And treated me
Like it was a job interview

Your poetry
Brags about how old school
You are
When I'll bet you aren't even 28

Your poetry
Is always depressing
It never shows any other emotion
But sadness

Your poetry
Reminds me of your boyfriend
They both can't handle their liquor
Or a little change

#1433

Your Everything

I fell asleep
During your one hundredth
Scorned woman routine
I drifted off
During your one hundredth
Lost love routine
Everyone has been scorned
Everyone has lost a love
Everyone is lonely
Your everything
Is just like everybody else's
For the one hundredth time

#1434

Plagiarist

Adults don't have to be
Serious all of the time
But what do you know
When they clapped for her
You got an idea
And when she wasn't around
You added a few "fucks"
And called "her's"
"Your's"
I am tired of you
And your posturing
I can only hope
That you are never published
Or even ever get the balls
To D.I.Y. it

#1435

Stood Up

I spit at you
In the last semester of high school
Because you bailed on me
When times were tough for me
One of your friends
Stood me up
On the last day of school
Before the Christmas break
We were supposed to go walking
In the square at night
Amongst the light covered trees
When I called to pick you up
Your mother said that you weren't home
I had that on my shoulders
All Christmas break
After the break
Back in school
You gave me a card
To placate me I guess
It did <u>not</u> work
I was a broken hearted
17 year old
I never dated a girl again
Until I was 21 years old
She was my first
And then she was my last
And she broke my heart too
And you wonder why
I never let women into my life
And you wonder why
I have been celibate for 10 years
And you wonder why
I spit at you
It is all because

I dreamt of getting
My heart broken
And it became
A self fulfilling prophecy
And I became
A grown up
17 year old

#1436

Don't Remember My Name

The bright spots
In your work
Are NOT few and
Far between
The bright spots
In your work
Don't exist
It is like you
And your work
Are stuck in junior high school
And your personality
Is just as petty
Oh
And by the way
That day you nearly hit
A guy
In your new car
Your new yellow
Convertible Mustang
(That I am quite sure
Your rich parents paid
At least partially for)
That guy was me
I guess your driving skills
Are stuck in junior high too
While you still won't remember
My name

#1437

High School Grad

While all of my friends
Went to the prom
Or
Went to get loaded
Or
Went to the prom
To get loaded
Or
Went to get loaded
To the prom
I went to bed
It was supposed to be
A happy day
But some guy in the audience yelled
"Get off the stage skinhead!"
The wind came out of my sails
So that when a friend said
"Smile Corey!"
I couldn't wait to get home
And got to sleep

While all of my friends
Were recovering from hangovers
I was working in a warehouse
Trying to forget yesterday's
"Happy day"

#1438

Crumbling Hope

I saw you today
You were 7 months pregnant
I had hoped that you wouldn't see me
But you did
And we talked uncomfortably
For what seemed
An eternity to me
But in reality
Was about 5 minutes
Then we went our separate ways
You had made promises
To me
To pay me for some photography
To buy a painting off of me
Etc., etc., etc.
None came true
So instead of getting angry at you
I chose to hope
Hope that I don't ever
Run into you again
The hope falls apart
Whenever I see you
And after I go home
To write about you
And then hope comes back again
But I know this is a small city
And my hope
Will probably crumble again and again

#1439

Fall Though

Even my sure things
Somehow
Fall through
Never enough
To put out my own work
Never enough
Coming in to support
Myself and my work
The silence is
Just as bad as violence
I shut my eyes
And hope that I can sleep
Through this
Sleep this off
And then
Hopefully the next day
Something
Finally
Works out
Instead of falling through

#1440

Sadder Than Leonard Cohen

I never had five million dollars
To steal
I never had a buddhist monastery
Consider me a flop
I never had a classical music store
Burn to the ground in a riot

But
I am still sad
Sadder than Leonard Cohen

#1441

Another No

I'm flattered but
No coast to coast for me
It is all below seasonal
Never returning my calls
Coming up with excuses
Spending at least one more day
Alone with myself and my art
Alone with myself at work
Alone with myself
I just wanted to get to work
And not deal with my property management
Because you can hear virtually everything
That makes a tired skin regenerate
And that gets me up at 4:30 in the morning
And comes and goes at 1:30 in the morning
And you find that the defendant
Will prevail
Because when the tents go up
I go down

#1442

And You Without Me

Even when I don't hear from you
For months
You are still on my mind
While I have painted myself
Into my corner of the room
I know
I know
I know
I know now I will see you
When I least expect it
And then
You could send half of me
Away
And I would still
Be all there
When you showed up
Even though
You smoke and drink
And who knows what else
I will work my way through
And you
You will continue to breath
Without me

#1443

My Right, Your Left

I sit at a bus stop
In the rain
My right
Your left
I tell you that
I am not interested
And you scurry away
Why do I always
Come so early for buses?
Because I don't want to be late
That's why I guess
Have I ever told you that
I miss you?
I don't remember if I have
Or not
And you don't remember either
My first book is called
Simply enough
"Keep Left"
But people are swayed
From buying it
Because they think
It is politics that it represents
They are half right
And half wrong
It is about personal politics
Not the politics of the suits
In the capital
But the politics of love
And hate
And guilt
And remorse
And even stronger passions
Than those of the suits in the capital

I sit at a bus stop
In the rain
My left
Your right
Hoping that some day
You will see through
The fancy titles and packaging
And open up with me
And my personal politics

#1444

People And Guns

The guns
Came up with a new way
Of killing people
And the people
Just kept dying

The guns
Just kept dying
While the people
Came up with new ways
Of killing themselves

The people
Come up with new ways
Of killing themselves
And the guns
Just kept killing

The people
And the guns
Just kept on killing themselves
While the war
Kept on raging

The war and the guns
Came up with new ways
Of killing people
And the people
Just kept dying

No one knows how it got started
Whether the guns or the war did
Most likely it was the people
And it will never end

Unless the people want it to

#1445

And I Am

I was beaten up
Yesterday
Just like every other day
Now it is today
And I am
Battered and bruised
Putting hope and blind faith
Into my paper
My voice
My canvas
My film
So you all
Keep coming back for more
And laughing at me
And not with me
All along
I should have known
All along

Yesterday at work
You sat with me
To eat your lunch
You are so young
And beautiful
That you give me strength
To laugh at my enemies
And my bruises disappear
And the laughter
Rebounds off of me
Like water off of a duck's back
Making me hope
That you like my work
And you find something
You have

In common with me
And I would be
Given the strength to move on

#1446

Around You

It's a broken poem
It's a broken method
It's a broken rhythm
Whenever I see you
I asked if you were
In high school
You told me
You are going for
Your Bachelor of Arts
At University
I feel lost around you
And I have lost my words
Around you
You are so young and beautiful
That I can't handle it
When it is late at night
And I will be around
This is all so repetitive
That my radio
Burns brightly
With all of my work
Following suit
And me just feeling old
And fat
And like an oddball with my tattoos
And
All
Used
Up
And
Old
This is a broken poem
For you and your youth
And me and my aged shyness

#1447

The Other Day

I got so excited
About talking to you
The other day
That I couldn't sleep last night
I had dreams
Of talking with you some more
Of being your friend
Of being your lover
Of never leaving your side
Of obsessing over someone
Who was nice to me once
For once
For once and for all
And about what he said
About you
Just to let you know
It disturbs me
To no end
Why would you want to
Pound a delicate flower?
I am such a pussy
That I got so excited
About you
That I can't stop
Thinking about you
And I hope you are nice
To me again
And again and
To no end

#1448

Too Personal

I have been told
That my work is too personal
One
Your work can never be
"Too personal"
Two
If your work isn't personal
Then you should quit
And three
All of you
Who say that my work
Is "too personal"
Are just jealous
That you don't have the brass balls
To put yourself on display
Like I do

Yesterday at work
I said that
You should call me
On your day off
You said that
"You would play it by ear"
I asked you
If you still had my number
You looked away from me
And said, "Yes."
You lied
I hate liars
That will be
The last time I approach you

You said that
You would like to

Go out with me
But never returned my calls
If you never
Wanted to go out with me
Then just tell me
If you aren't attracted to me
Then just tell me
I would have respect for you
For being honest
Instead you are a liar
And I hate liars

How is that, fools?
Is that "too personal" enough for you?

#1449

I Am Always Sorry

I hope
That I didn't offend you
By calling you a "delicate flower"
Having a crush on you
Pulls out the romantic in me
So I am sorry
If I offended you

Isn't it amazing
How friends can turn on you
When you need them the most?
Leaving you wondering
What you did wrong
And slightly bitter too
Maybe I shouldn't be sorry now

Got nothing
Won't go too far
My heart is strained
And in flames
All at once
Making me wonder
Will I be alone forever?

Dream me over to you
Make sure no evil follows
And let us hope
That this dream
Comes true
And we never part
Even if it is just friends

#1450

Back In The Box

I don't like your writing
Or your politically charged girlfriend
Who always asks me out to shows
Seeing you two together
Makes me think of junior high school
And how out of place I felt
Your girlfriend reminds me of this girl
In grade 8 that I had a crush on
Once she asked me if I ever wanted to
You know?
Had I ever thought about
Having sex with her?
And to be honest
I was 14
And hadn't even masturbated yet
So I told her no
She then started to describe
Naked scenarios with me
Two weeks later
I asked her out
She said no
And that she had a boyfriend already
Sorry
I got off topic
I am too sensitive
I should let things
Wash off of me
But I can't
I am tired of boxes
And circle jerks
And lying
And back biting
And being placated to
I don't fit in with you

Your girlfriend
Or your girlfriend's mom
I don't drink
I don't smoke
I don't do drugs
And I
And I
And I don't care anymore
And I want to go to sleep
And never wake up

#1451

Waste Your Time On Me

Hello there
I see you every time I come in
This is the only way I see you
And sometimes
I wish that it would never end
This darkness gets to me
I wish you would
Take me home
Or
Come home with me
We could just watch movies
Or listen to music
Or
Just
Talk
But something inside me
Tells me
That you wouldn't
Waste your time on me
I wish that I could believe in heaven
Or a god
But what god
Would let this terrible place
Continue being a terrible place
And
If I believed that there was a heaven
I would have killed myself
Minutes after my Grandfather Hamilton's funeral
Sorry
So
Sorry
For getting off topic
I just thought that
I would let you know
Every time I see you
I miss you

#1452

I am more scared
Of open doors
Than closed doors
Closed doors
Can sometimes hold
Opportunity
And prove a fear invalid
Open doors
Can sometimes show
I am wrong
And show me that my fear is justified

#1453

Chaos In The Court

I showed you my latest book
You looked semi-impressed
And said that you weren't interested in buying
Suddenly
I felt old
And detached from the place
Where I work
I wanted to go home
And set myself on fire

You said that you weren't interested in buying
Just writing your own
I should have kept
My mouth shut
And my life to myself
Serves me right
To get a crush
On a girl
A young girl

#1454

Hypocrite

I think of suicide
My suicide
All of the time
Matter of factly
But when I hear
A friend's friend did it
It makes me sad
Especially when they are young
And full of potential
I feel burnt out
Not being able to express
Myself properly to anyone
Except myself
I end up getting in shit
And wishing even more
That I was dead
And that no one else
Should wish this
Knowing that I am a hypocrite
Hoping we all live life to the fullest
Before we all go to pieces
I am sorry
For being so wrong

#1455

My Blood Is Pumping

She sat down
At the table
With the young handsome guy
Instead of mine
I suddenly felt old
Of course I should have known
Youth goes with youth
And age
And age by itself
With its pot belly
And grey in its beard
Listening to its Neil Young records

My eyes drifted to the window
And saw the street below
Hoping that I would have a quick death
Falling out of a high rise
Getting hit by a train
Overdosing on my medications
Not wanting to turn around
And see her beautiful youth
With his handsome youth
Enjoying themselves
While I sat at a table alone and
On fire

#1456

Another Lost Number

You want to be the hero
But you don't realize that
Everyone wants to be the hero
At some point in their life
The knight in shining armor
The soldier to to raise the flag at Iwo Jima
The doctor to find the cure for Cancer
Etc.
Etc.
Etc.
If you only want to be around me
In times of trouble
Then why should I accept you at all
If you won't be visible in the good times?
I don't need another hero
I am my own hero
My small circle of friends are my heroes too
Because they are there for me
Good and bad
And I am there for them
In good or bad
If you don't want friendship
Then tell me
I would have respect for you
Instead you beat around the bush
Being the diplomat
To everyone's broken parts
Do you know what happens
To these type diplomats in the end?
They are buried alive
By their lack of honesty
Do you know what happens
To your type of hero in the end?
They are written about

Until the years ravage the pages
And then everyone forgets their name
Only to remember it
Once they are playing a game of trivia
I want more staying power
Than that
I want to be and breathe
And bleed and eat
My own personal hero
And keep my friends
Who have been there
For better or for worse
For the eventual lottery win
I love my friends
My acquaintances are disposable
I love some of my family
The rest are disposable
I have staying power
You never will
Being a self help book
In the discount bin
Of your oneness hero

#1457

Humbling Weather

Ring the alarm
Winter is on her way
To make us all
More humble
Put away the short shorts
Put away the Fall Classic
And bring on the Cup
School's in
And we all hunker down
For a winter that is long
Longer than a long lonely night
Of a 40 year old man
Who has never kissed a woman
Or even a girl
Maybe I should listen to Bob Dylan
More or less?
Maybe I should listen to Slayer
Less or more?
Ring the alarm
Winter is on her way
To give us all humility

#1458

Keep On Running

I keep on saying
"I won't fuck it up this time"
And in the end
I do fuck it up anyways
Somehow I always do
It is like some big joke
I think
That even if I moved away
Far away from here
I would still have
The money pains
The artistic growing pains
The loneliness
And no lover
Why would some woman
Any woman want
And/or need me?
All I have to offer are
Lots of books
Lots of music
Lots of my own art
And myself
And the women
Keep on saying
"It is not enough
Because you keep on fucking up"

#1459

Winter Dreams

Just before I woke up
This morning
I dreamt
That it was the first snow fall
Of the year
And I was back in my parent's house
Peering out my bedroom window
At the street outside
Not worried that I had no winter clothing
Yet
The leaves hadn't fully fallen off
Yet
I couldn't stop thinking about you
And the gentle curves of your body
And your bright blue eyes
That sometimes seemed to match
The blue in my eyes
And the blue in the sky outside
Which was one of the few things
We have in common
We both have tattoos
And we both have similar tastes in music
But that is where the similarities end
You drink
And smoke
And
And
I miss you
Like I miss my winter clothing
On the first day of snow
And now as I rub my eyes
I realize that it was all just a dream

#1460

Photographs Of A Crush

I had crushes
On two women
With the same first name
But it never worked out
One of them moved away
To the coast
And the other
Always says that she will call me
But never does
This all makes me very sad

I had crushes
On two women
With the same first name
But it never worked out
It never does
So I took pictures of them
When we were still friends
So when my memory fades
I will still have a keepsake
This all makes me very sad

Because it never works out for me

#1461

About Them

I want to do what is right
And quit running around
All blurry eyed
About the past
So much so
That I can't see
What is in front of me
It is not them
Because I just can't write
About them
The way she does

Saying "who cares?"
After reading
Clean yourself up
Constantly
Change your style
Constantly
(Here is a dig)
Quit criticizing me
I don't do it to you (unless provoked)
So why do it to me?
I just want to do what's right

I just want to do what's right
But I am still a hypocrite

#1462

Avarice

Is it me?
Or is it you?
Is it greedy
To want you all of the time
Or not at all?
Is it me?
Or is it you?
I am looking
For the reason
You don't return
My call
And I emphasize call
Because you said
You would
And never did
Is it me?
Or is it you?
I called you once
That is why I emphasize call
And you never returned my call
And I am left wondering
Is it me?
Or is it you?

#1463

Cherish

It had been cloudy all week
Then
Today
The sun broke loose
From its hazy shackles
And shone
And I heard
Lawn mowers
Children getting off of buses
People walking and chatting
And I thought
If it could last forever
But then it clouded over
Again
To remind me it was
Nearly winter
And the days were shorter
So I cherished
That brief moment of sunlight
And wrote this all down
To remind me that
Winter is not forever
A beautiful memory is

#1464

Burn, Shoot And Loot My Dreams

My dreams in last night's sleep
Haunt me even now
With the morning almost over
Tanks patrolling the streets
Of the town I grew up in
Gunfire in the shopping mall
Parking lot at night
A calm goth woman
Chatting with me about love
The next part of the dream
The goth woman
Had lost the gothic
And let her natural hair colour grow back
And was wearing a parka and jeans
She was tired of looking depressed
She thought she could
Hide her depression
With bright clothes
She still sounded depressed
But looked just as beautiful
As before
Then there were spies
Who we found out
And shot on the spot
To be made examples of
I was hired
To dispose of their vehicles
Burn, shoot and loot
I was so sick yesterday
And I always dread
The sickness dreams
They haunt me
For days
After the sickness leaves

#1465

Jammed Out On

My younger
More successful artist sister
Told me
"Van Gogh never sold a painting
Now look at him,
He is an icon"
But he killed himself
He is a dead icon
I want to be a living icon
Or at least make a living

My younger
More successful artist sister
Told me
"Nick Drake overdosed on anti-depressants
Because no one listened,
Now lots of people listen"
But he killed himself
It was all
Too little, too late
He is a dead icon too

I truly believe
If you do not understand
The fragility and insecurity of an artist's life
And if you do not fully understand
Why suicide was an option
Then you will never grasp
What it is like to struggle
With inner demons
And without respect all of your life
And you will most certainly
Never grasp the magnitude
Or strength of the artist's work

#1466

Don't be a runaway
Survive
And destroy
Destroy tradition
Destroy bigotry
Destroy stereotypes
Destroy negativity
Don't run away
From the blackness
Survive it
Learn from it
And then
Destroy it

#1467

Shake Down

We kissed
For what seemed like hours
Days
Months
Years
You then said
"Let's have a sleep over"
But I was so wired
That I couldn't sleep
So I went home
With you in my thoughts
Your taste in my mouth
And your smell on my clothes
I can't help but feel
It is going much too fast
But also that I have been set free
From my 10 year prison sentence
I miss you already
And it has been only days
Hours
Minutes
Seconds
Since I last saw you
And shorter since
I last talked to you
I have been set free
I just hope that
My struggling passion
And my ongoing loneliness
Doesn't swallow you whole
Like my mouth did
Over your tongue

#1468

I Have Run Out Of Patience

She said
"Let's just be friends
So no more kissing"
How come no one ever says
"Let's just be lovers"
I will never know the answer
To that one
She said
"I have no regrets"
I wanted to say
"I do"
Had I known
That the "friend" card
Was going to be pulled
I wouldn't have kissed you
Not even once
Can you keep a secret?
I wish that I had never
Kissed a girl
Who just wanted to be friends
I wish that I had never
Had sex with a girl
Who dumped me
Or never loved me
I wish that I was still a virgin
This whole poem
Brings out the sadness in me
The suicidal thoughts
Start bubbling to the surface
The depression that lasts for months
Comes out in seconds
I have so much to regret
And it will never end
Until I am six feet under

#1469

Maybe Next Time: Part 2

It was a fall
Full of fear
It was a near winter
Full of sadness
Tonight
I will have a 2 hour
Shower to cleanse my skin
Of your smell
But I know
Deep in my heart
My memory will betray me
And I will swear
That I smell you
All around my home
I always say
"I won't fuck it up
This time"
But I always do
And deep in my heart
I know how bad
I wanted it to work out
But it just got worse
Before it got better
And I'll
I'll
I'll
I will
Maybe next time
I will get it right
Maybe next time

#1470

Days Later

You can never tell
Anyone
Anything
I have learned that
From you and him
I have also learned that
You can say no to men
But that you can't say no to pets
You can say that
You want me badly
But then push me away
Days later
You have never said that
You needed me
And you push me away
Not knowing that
I am on your side
Even though,
To quote Hank Williams Sr.
"I am so lonesome I could cry"
I must be the loneliest boy
In the whole land
But I will keep all of this
To myself
Because you can never tell
Anyone
Anything

#1471

Counting The Hours

I trust you enough
To let you sleep
In my home
While I am at work
Counting the hours
I have faith in you
That you will be there
When I get home
After I finished
Counting the hours
And I hope
That we will be able to hug
And that it won't hurt much
That I was away
Counting the hours
We will be relieved
That I am home
And the little things
Will count
Like the count down
At work until
The gentle kisses
The loving words
And more
I trust you
And I trust that you believe me
When I say
I love you
Even when I am
Counting the hours

#1472

The First Time I Tried Viagra

I hope that we can last
A little while longer
I am not sure
If you believe me
When I say
"It will all work out"
Let the phone ring
We are too busy to answer
You patiently take me
And my lonesome body
In your hands
And your patience
Makes me love you more
And the next time that we are apart
I miss you more than
At the beginning
And the next time that we are apart
I love you all the more
And when we are finished
And I have been complete
And whole
For the first time
You tell me that
You would love me
Even without the love making
I hope that we can last
A little while longer
Because it will all work out
And then hopefully
We can last
A lot longer

#1473

Sensitive Mediocrity

I want to escape
From this sea of mediocrity
And say what I feel
And feel what I say
Negative or positive
And hear what people feel
About me
Negative or positive
If you want to say it
Say it
Feel it
Know it
If I respect you
Then I know that it is right
Negative or positive
If you are too sensitive
Then maybe you should quit
This war
War of words
War of wits
War of love
All is fair in a war of love
All is fair in
Love and war
All is fair
When those who have shot me
Get shot back by me
And I will continue to shoot
Until I escape
From this sea of sensitive mediocrity

#1474

Smile, It Is The Future Dammit

You say
"I don't care,
I just really do not"
But you do really care
So you are a hypocrite
If you say
"I don't care,
I just really do not"
When you do care
So much so in fact
You tell me
Not to say anything
Critical
About the sensitive artists
Who all need thicker skin
You are like a Republican
Who needs thicker skin
Freedom of speech
Only if you are not
Critical
Of the Republican president
Who needs thicker skin
I have seen the future
Everyone is just good
No one is bad
And no one needs to be better
And everyone is smiling
No one is in ear shot
No one needs help
Everyone is mediocre
I have seen your future
And it is a circle jerk
One that I don't want to be a part of
And it is also a future of hypocrites

That I don't want to be part of
This is <u>your</u> future
You bleeding heart liberal hypocrite
You think that I am the only one
In critical condition?
Sensitive artist?
A mediocre future
Where no one critiques anyone
If this is the future
Then I would rather be alone
Again

#1475

My Time Is Almost Done

You can run all of your life
But believe me
When I say to you
I heard Johnny Cash say
"God is going to cut you down"
I don't believe in a god
But I believe Johnny
I believe what I heard
Because I saw the sky turn red
The meek shall inherit the shit
And I await for my time
To come and assign my future
Before he comes to cut me down
I yell for all to hear that
"It is better to reign in hell
Than to serve in heaven!"
But I am not a religious man
But I believe it
When Mr. Cash says
My time is almost done
Time is not on my side
So my work must be quick
And as accurate as a sniper's bullet
I have run far too long
It is now time to face my future
And as long as I have a little time
Then it will all fall into place

#1476

Archives

I was never a lover
I was never a bank robber
I was never a murderer
Or a rapist
Or a racist
Or a fence sitter
At 14 a girl that I had a crush on
Asked me if
I wanted to have sex with her
I hadn't even masturbated yet
So my answer was
No
She described what she
Would do to me
If given the chance
Weeks later
We went to the prom together
I got so worked up
That I was sick in the washroom
For most of the evening
The next day
I asked her out
She said
No
And that was the last time
That I talked to her
Now
I am seeing a woman
Who wants to have my baby
I am so intimidated by her
That I feel like I am 14 again
But she means well
I am not so sure whether
The girl when I was 14 meant well

High school was a little different
I was still buried and bullied
But the girls came onto me
Because I drank too much
And drugged too much
And that was trendy at the time
But I was blind to them
Except for the girl who
Sucked me off in the back room
For some reason
I couldn't walk properly
For 2 days afterwards
She then spread rumors
That I was seeing her
And later on I told her off in a bar
And she threw an ashtray
At my head
I was 14 all over again
Damn
I wish that I had not smoked
All that hash
And did all those mushrooms
I think of Gillian Welch's song
"My First Lover"
When I think of my first lover
I was 21 and had never fucked before
And I didn't smoke, drink, drug
Or even do caffeine
And when I was finished
She said that she loved me
But I still felt 14 all over
Especially
When she dumped me
In the shower
Now I am seeing someone
Who is so patient with me
That I have to pinch myself
Ahhh

New love
And so far
I don't feel 14 again

#1477

Words

It should never have to do
Because I always get by
Now I see all of those people
Those comfortable people at work
As being smarter than me
They are comfortable
I am struggling to get by
And leave it to me
To help you out
And help myself out
For once
Now I can say it bravely
I want more for myself
And more for you
And more for us
But I am a restless soul
After I leave marks on your neck
I am your prey
But I don't mind
I am a willing victim
And you are my willing captor
But I don't mind
One bit
I miss you so much
I always get by
With my restless soul
And you are there
With me
With or without fortunes

#1478

Pin On

You have a gift inside you
And we shall make it
A home
Where no one thought
Would be possible
With us
You have a gift inside you
And I pray to a higher power
(I know that I don't usually do that)
That I won't fuck things up
Between you
And I
That I won't fuck things up
Between the child on the way
And you
And I
I love you dearly
And I couldn't think of
A better place to be
On New Year's eve
Than with you
Making an otherwise
Dreary tradition
Special

this piece was written
on December 31, 2006
in Edmonton

#1479

With My Child

And to think I loved you

The night I was dumped
By a christian
Because I was an Atheist
Because of my illness
Because of my finances
I heard other people's conversations
Clear as a bell
She was pregnant
With our child
With my child
With her child
And told me
(In a rehearsed manner)
She never loved me
And she was selfish
To want a child
And was going to put the child
Up for adoption
In a good christian home
A home that believed in god
A home that would be better
Than our's would be
And that I had no rights
Concerning our child
My child
Her child
I felt anger at this
But most of all
I wanted to die
But that her family probably
Brainwashed her
I am sure her family

Would like me to go that way
But I will live on
To be a thorn in her side
And their side

And to think I loved you

#1480

Tell Me

Don't tell me
You love me
Then 4 months later
Tell me
That you never did

Don't tell me
You don't want
Any contact
And then give me your
Mother's phone number
To pass messages to

Don't tell me
You want to have my baby
And then when
You are pregnant
You tell me
You don't want me
To see the baby

Don't tell me
You want to marry me
Then drop me
Like a hot potato
When you see me
Depressed for the first time

Don't tell me
Lies
Because they hurt
A million times more
Than the truth

Don't tell me
I have a big heart
When you break it
And make me feel like
My heart is a big target

Just tell me
It will work out
Just tell me something
Like Bob Marley said
"Every little thing
Will work out"
I really hope that it will
Because I am running out
Of hope

Just tell me
That there is hope

#1481

No Religion, No War

I said that
There is no justice
In this world
He said
that is why we have religion
I felt like saying
That is what got me into this mess
In the first place dickwad
I was seeing a slack christian girl
But her family wasn't slack
Her family seemed to have brainwashed her
And now I have a kid on the way
That I will never see in person
Because I am an Atheist
Christians preach tolerance
But very rarely practice it
And that is why there is no justice
In this world
Because if there was no religions
I am confident
That there would be no war or prejudice
Just love and justice

#1482

I understand dying
Maybe too much
Maybe so much so
That I forget about living

#1483

Beauty And The Beast

The other day
My pregnant girlfriend and I
Were standing on a crowded bus
And some mentally challenged guy
Hit my ass 4 times
As my girlfriend and I were getting off
I swatted him in the face
And put my face in his
And said mockingly
"Sorry"
While we were walking
Away from the stop
Some other guy asked me
What that was for
I told him that
That guy hit my ass 4 times
And we walked away
Towards the hospital

This reminded me
Of the time I went to a movie
With my first girlfriend
I was looking forward
To seeing this movie
During the movie 3 guys and 1 girl
Were making a bunch of noise
Throughout the movie
People complained
But nothing stopped them
Except when I finally
Lost my cool and
Stood up and yelled
"Why don't you all just
Shut the fuck up!

Some people are
The stupidest motherfuckers!"
Everyone clapped
And the four went silent
My first girlfriend and I soon broke up

Back to the present
My girlfriend and I
Were sitting in a hospital
Waiting to see what the
Problem was with her pregnancy
My nerves were frazzled
But I felt like
I had embarrassed her
So I apologized for hitting the guy
In the face
Because he hit my ass 4 times
She said that it was OK
Except maybe he liked my ass
That maybe he was sexually attracted
To my fat ass
Or "M.F.A." as I like to call it
I think M.F.A. would make a great band name
"Hello (your city of choice)! We are M.F.A.!"
Anyways
Maybe he liked me
And he was the beauty
And I
And I was the beast

#1484

The Seams

I struggled with this
For hours
For days
For weeks
And when it finally came
To fruition
I could barely breathe
And you stared blankly
Into my eyes
My eyes
Which you always liked
Because they were so blue
Now you talk to me
As if nothing happened
When I feel as if
My world has split
At the seams

The next day
I still struggled with it
Even though
You treated me poorly
Now the oceans
Have all dried up
And the trees
Have all died
And there are still
Stains on the walls
Of my apartment
And the air I breathe
Is dry and stale
When I realize
We won't touch
Flesh on flesh

Ever again

#1485

The Gentle Way

I met Steve almost 23 years ago
When I was about 12 years old

I was constantly getting
Beat up and made fun of at school
When my Dad suggested Judo
Because he wanted to take it as a kid
But there was no one teaching it
In a small rural town in Manitoba
When it piqued his interest

He took me to the Sherwood Park Judo Club
And I met Fumiko (Steve's wife)
And Steve Fukushima
Here's a little background on Steve
He was born and raised
In Richmond, B.C.
His mother and father immigrated
To Canada
In the 1920's to 1930's
And they bought a house and a fishing boat

When Steve was about 10 or 11
World War 2 started and everything changed
His family was rounded up
And placed in P.O.W. camps
Near Lethbridge, Alberta I believe
And he spent the next few years there
When he was released
And they went back to Richmond
Some white people owned it
And their boat was gone
Without even seeing a picture of Japan
Steve and his family

Moved to Japan
All his siblings and parents
Refused to have anything to do with Canada
Steve never told me why he came back
He just shrugged his shoulders
I remember when Mulroney
Apologized to the Japanese-Canadians
Steve basically said
Too little, too late

Back to his Judo club
After a few years
I began gaining confidence
And the beatings all but stopped
By the time I got my brown belt
(One step below a black belt)
I had even fought my way out
Of a 2 on one situation

When Steve moved back to Canada
He settled in Ottawa
And taught at the Takahashi Judo Club
Which was one of the best in Canada
Years later when he came to Edmonton
With the Consulate General of Japan
He opened up his club in Sherwood Park
The back of his gy still said "Takahashi"
One lady with a son in the club
Kept on calling him "Mr. Takahashi"
I finally told her he was Steve Fukushima
And that he just didn't want to make waves
She still asked him why
He just shrugged his shoulders
And said in his broken English that
"It was OK I don't mind"

Now I am 35 and
Steve and I talk a couple of times

A year
But one week before Christmas
Every year
My call display says "Weber Motors"
I know that it is Steve
Because he has bought 2 cars from there
And that he is wanting to take me out
To A & W for a coffee and a chat
Steve
Helped me with my confidence
And became a good friend to me
When I needed one
This poem is a thank you
To Steve
To let him know that I love him
And no matter what happens
We will always be friends
Thanks again Steve

#1486

Don't Try, Just Don't

Don't try and think about her
It will drive you crazy
I mean
She will drive you crazy
I try to write more
Paint more
Photograph more
But I usually end up
Laying in bed
Missing her smell
Her touch
Her breath on my neck
Her taste in my mouth
I think to myself that
I would rather
Set myself on fire
Than miss her so badly
I would rather
Close my eyes
And never open them again
Than miss all of the fun we had
Starting tomorrow
I will forget her name
I will forget my name
Sleep for days
And when I wake up
I will not think about her
And all of the fun we had
I will just move on
No matter how hard it is
I will move on

#1487

Ink And Paper Hope

I am putting all of my hope
Into ink and paper
Into paint and canvas
Waiting for the "big break"
To come along
Does everyone get a "big break?"
Or do some get it
But just miss it?
Did I just miss it
Sometime in my past?
Did I miss my "big break?"
And now I am wandering blindly
Waiting for lightning
To strike a second time?
I would tend to say
That lightning
Never strikes twice
But I heard a song in the 80's
That said never say never
I would like to think
That if my "big break" came along
I would seize the day
As it were
And better my position
In life
In my life
And in my head

#1488

I Have No Doubt

I have no doubt
About it
My so called talents
That I feel in my inner core
I will eventually get by on them
And not use my disability crutch
To support myself
I dream about not needing
My head doctors
And my pills
My so called talents
Taking over the reigns
Of therapy
Of my therapy
It will stay a dream
Because I have no doubt
That it is not possible
For pen and paper
To replace shrinks
For paint and canvas
To replace pills
But financially
I know
I have no doubt
About it
That it will
That my finances will
All work out
I have no doubt
About this at all

#1489

A Scar On A Scar

I have tattoos
Over top of
Self mutilation scars
I have scars
On top of
Scars
Her ghost
Makes me wish that
My phone would ring
Makes me want
To cut myself open
For all to see
My insides out
While I think to myself that
I just have to learn
How to breath again
But it is hard to learn again
When it feels like
Such a loss
To me
When it is a loss
To her
That's what everyone
Tells me anyways
It still hurts
It still hurts my scars
It still hurts my tattoos
It still hurts

#1490

On Liars

I don't need anymore lies
Or liars
The truth hurts
But the pain is worth it
No pain
No gain
But the lies
Are a brick wall in my path
A wall bigger
Than that one in China
Or that one
Around your lying heart
I don't need anymore lies
Or liars
Back in the days
That you thought it was
A good photo op
It was actually a faulty truss
That came down
On your head
Photo op
The lie
The false truss
The truth
If you don't get this now
Then you never will

#1491

About It

It makes no difference to me
But it does to you
So much so
You choose to push me out
Of your life
On Valentine's Day
Your reasons
Are irrelevant
Your actions
Are reprehensible
And the fact that
You have no conscience
About it
Leaves me dreading
The day we met
The night we slept together
This makes a difference
To me
Now I find it easy
To fall back into old ways
And not trust anyone
Except for myself

#1492

Least

Haul out your eyes
It is easy
If you try
Keep a diary of sadness
Pull it out
Only at small gatherings
Or parties
Take your eyes
And diary
To the bus
It will take you
Some place better
You hope anyways
You have to change
But change only comes
When you let go
When you get there
Give me a call
When you release
When you find a release
When you release
Your extra baggage
I know you carry
Why look at the past
When it is not profitable
To do so
So put in your new eyes
Throw out your old diary
And start a new one
And don't forget
To give me a call
When you do
Because I will be waiting
With open arms

To congratulate you
It is the least I can do

#1493

Never Cry After Her

She never cried
Or showed any emotion
When she said
That she never loved me
So I never cried
Or showed any emotion either
It all ended
On Valentine's Day
For good
Now I like
Valentine's Day even less
Than before
And now I like
Her about as much as a leper
She is not worthy of me
And my
Integrity
Loyalty
Honor
And honesty
I will give her a wide berth
And never cry again
Crying was history
Before her
And will stay that way
After her

#1494

Get Me Out Of Here

No
I don't drink alcohol
No
I don't do drugs
No
I don't fuck around
So
If you ask me one more time
I will punch you in the face
I want to be free
Just not <u>your</u> freedom
You follow
And chase
At the same time
I walk side by side
With my freedom
I quit stealing fire
Back in the early 90's
When I turned into a mean drunk
With all of the alcohol
When I got bored
With the drugs
And the fuck thing
Well that's for me to know
And you to never find out
Unless you are my friend
And you and your weaknesses
Are not my friends
And never were
And never will be
Now
Get me out of here
Now

#1495

Hate Myself To Love You

You are so sure that
I will fall in love with you eh?
You with your mediocrity
And your bitterness
It would be a major faux paus
To sit with me
Wouldn't it?
So go sit with your aliens
And discuss
How estranged you feel
From everyone else around you
The funny thing is
All of your alien friends
Say the exact same thing
You do
When you are not around
No
I won't fall in love with you
I would have to hate myself
To love you

#1496

Stress Release

Building up steam
To knuckle down
And finally get it
Out of the way
So I am no longer
A part of it
I will kiss you on the lips
If you want
Smell your breath
Taste your tongue
Feel you breathing in
And out
I should be used to it by now
But in some sense
I am still a virgin
And even though
You are so much younger
Than me
You are most likely
The wiser one of
The two of us
Maybe
I should shut my mouth
And let this crush
Live on
Like a lottery ticket
That you haven't checked
To see if you won
Or not
I picture myself
Asking you out
To a function
And you giving me
A soft no

So as not to hurt me
Too much
I guess it is for the better
Just let me go
And I will let off
Some steam
In this wish list of mine
Until someone
Works out with me
Knuckle down
It could be awhile
Yes
It could be a very long time
Or no
Be positive
It could happen in 20 minutes
And we could
Do the happily
Ever after
Knuckle down
I have my work
Cut out for me

#1497

With Your Writing

In your writing

Take no prisoners
Aim for the heart first
Then the head
After that
All of the other senses
Will follow

Forget about performing
Your written words
Should pierce
Like a bullet
To the head
And they should be just as fast
If not faster

Hone your craft
Alone
Alone in your low rent
Apartment
Alone in a bar
Alone in a library
Alone on a bus
Just make sure that you are alone

Never write drunk on anything
It dulls your senses
And when you are writing
That is when you
Need your senses most
If you become addicted
Your sense will fail you

And finally
Ignore everyone else
Around you
While you are writing
Because your craft
Should be the most important thing

In your life

#1498

Defeatist

I know full well
It won't work out
Even though
We are the same age
You are a successful
Business woman
And I am a failing
Artist
I do wish it would
Work out
For you seem
To know what you want
And in my little experience
That is rare to find
In a woman
Of any age
I guess
I should leave it
As a crush
And stick with
What I do best
My lonely
Defeatist art

#1499

Ode To The Young Hipsters

Take your green "Fidel Castro" hat
That covers your filthy dreadlocks
And shove it up your ass
Quit preening your hair
And, oh, by the way
Your 21 year old ass
Looks fat in that
50 year old dress
Don't get me wrong
I like earth tone sweaters
As much as the next guy
But when I see them
At every "hip" show
On every boy and girl
It makes me want to
Use a flame thrower
On your girlfriend's fat ass
And on you and your tattooed
Dreadlock covered shoulders
I saw three of you
That looked exactly the same
At the show last week
Maybe this shows my age
Maybe it is just me
But it is not what is on the outside
That counts
It is what is on the inside
That counts
And I am afraid to say
From what I have just witnessed
You are void of anything original
In both departments

#1500

At Peace

Trust the police
To arrest you
If you read one more poem
Chewing with your mouth open
Is all you are doing
Chewing on your cud
You are a well paid dictator
Of the crowd
That is why
I won't sit with you
A few weeks ago
My doctor
Cleaned my ears out
And 2 big chunks
Of wax
Came out
Now unfortunately
I hear you
Better than ever
The company owns the land
But you are still paying
For that car of your's
Macho appeal
For the men
A second glance
From the women
To see if you are
A middle aged man
Eventually
It will all catch up
To you
And the police
Will get you
And I will finally be

At peace

#1501

Bruised Audio

I've been waiting
For this silence
All my life
And it is not working
Out
I asked her if she painted
To find out
If she got in
To that big local show
She walked away irritated
Later at the end of our shifts
She smiled at me
As I walked toward
The elevator
I didn't smile back
I was being placated to
Now in the silence
Of an early spring night
I realize that
I enjoy the silence
It is more natural
Than being given
The cold shoulder
I have been waiting
For this silence
All of my life
And it is finally
Working out

#1502

Look Out

Look out
Above your head
Watching the monkey
Land on your back
Every Friday and Saturday night
Then you
Angry young man
Who can't handle his booze
Goes on the avenue
And starts a fight
Breaks a store window
Harasses the 24 hour store clerks
Whistle at the scantily clad
Women
And sometime girls
Look out
At the sometimes girls
Who never sometimes say no
When the alcohol is flowing
And when a 15 year old girl's
First sexual encounter
Gives her a S.T.D.
And a mother who kicks
Her out
And holds a grudge
Even when she is now 28
And you
You both
You three
You all get raped
Every weekend
And come Monday morning
It is the same story
In every city

With people
Who
Never
Look out

#1503

Just Ask

This regret
It kills
This loneliness
Immobilizes
If I could just
Dispose this fear
Then maybe
I would see you
In a different light
So I hold on
To a dream
And your smell
And your eyes
And your hair
And I hope
That this regret
Goes no further
Than my barren room
And the immobilizing
Loneliness passes
And this fear
I leave at the door
And I just ask

#1504

Consortium Of Expectations

I had a dream
Just moments ago
That a young hipster guy
I have met
Wrote something
While I was sleeping
With my first girlfriend
He used my name on it
And put it out
On the web
It was only 3 paragraphs
With an eye-catching photograph
Of a purple and yellow moon
It was so unique
And controversial
That people tried to kill me
Even as I tried to get him
A publishing deal
So I barricaded myself
Alone
In my apartment
Alone
Because my girlfriend left me
On Valentine's Day
And the young hipster guy left me
Frowning
Because I burned my first
50 poems
Even with this in mind
He left to praise me
To everyone
Eventually
After days of persuasion
I got him a publishing deal

And when he came back
I thought he was
Just another assassin
But he had come back
Just to see
How I was holding up
I was so excited to see him
To tell him
That I got him a publishing deal
But he rejected it all
Saying that
He was just trying
To get me
To provoke him
And others like him
Into creating their own
Unique brand of controversy
And he had succeeded
But was unwilling
To accept my gift
Because it compromised him
And the purple and yellow moon
(That was promised him
In the publishing deal
That I got him)
So he left
And again I had to clean up
And this time
Instead of waiting
For him and my first girlfriend
To come back
I went to sleep
For days
In perfect bliss
Because I knew
I had finally lived up to
Someone else's expectations
Besides my own

No matter
What the outcome

#1505

Yesterday

I saw you at the art gallery
Yesterday
And you just ignored me
You even looked at me
And my nametag
And looked the other way
The last time I saw you
I had the audacity to say
Hello
And you said that we would talk later
We never did
Because you ignored me
The rest of the evening
Then another time
You said you were busy
With a certain event on a
Certain day
In a certain place
I found out the next day
That this certain event
At this certain place
Was the day before
I wanted to go out with you
Now I am
Now my heart
Now my brain
Is full of hate
From all of these deceptions
And I just can't seem
To pass it off
And make it
Yesterday

#1506

Cheating Death

Kiss death
On the lips
And right before
You slip him the tongue
And right before
He sucks in
Your last breath
Knee him in the crotch
And walk away
As if nothing
Ever happened

#1507

Storms And Strangers

My poems
Are storms
My storms
Have numbers
And names
Today my numbers and names
And poems and storms
Are strangers screaming
At each other because
They can't make the rent
And they don't love each other
Anymore
And they are so lonely
No matter the number or name
They are so lonely
Because life never works out
How it is supposed to
And the grind
Is a sweet nothing
That fills your brain
With nothings
With poems
And storms
And numbers
And names

#1508

To Fall And To Leave

No good can come from this
Right to the very end
Even with
Known quality tested products
I should have known better
Than to trust you
There was an emergency summit
War planes shelling insurgents
Politicians seeking an end
To the current economic woes
I told you not to betray
All of these facts
But you went ahead
And did betray
Which left little room to wonder
Where your loyalties lie
Your loyalties lied
And I was the one
To fall
And you were the one
To leave

I should have known that
No good would have come from this

#1509

Cut Back Good Boy, Cut Back

Forced by depression
To reach the last hour
To reach and try to rise
But still sinking
In the mire
Of something I worked
Hard at
And got nothing for
Cut back
Be a good boy
Cut back
Be a good boy
The day I was told
About my rent increase
It snowed like mad
And in my apartment
It rained like sad
And I tried to be good
But I was irresponsibly bad
And in the moment of truth
I sunk
Like the rest who sunk
In the crusades
Forced down by depression
And loss
And she is so angry with me
And I don't know why
I was just trying to be friendly
And now
Forced by depression
I hastily retreat
To my home
Where I know
I know

What it is like to be alone
So much so
So much
So
So what
So what if
I went to sleep
And never woke up
So what
I am tired of being
Kicked in the balls
So much
So what
Cut back
I just have to
Cut back
So much
So what

#1510

Come On Over

I have been hearing the same things
All night long
So that when I hear my name
Passed around
I don't even turn around
I would like to meet you
Some place quiet
Where the young hipsters
With attitude problems
Are not to be found
I want to take you there
Kiss you on the lips
And hope that you return
The favor
But I just realized that
I was born for this
Born to lose
Born to walk away
With my tail between my legs
Born to hear my name
Passed around
But the buck for me
Is passed over
In favor of alcohol
Or smokes
Or dope
I can see food
But alcohol
And smokes
And narcotics
Well at least I still have my balls
For when I am confronted
About some silly disagreement
And then the next day

My balls get kicked in
By some bitch with an axe to grind
Well
Guess what?
My balls always come back
And as long as
You don't pass over my name
Or embarrass me in public
Then I will never
Pass over you and your smile

#1511

Feeling Now

The traffic is so weak now
That I can write freely
And not have to worry
About screwing up
Another word
And not have to worry
About getting pity
From another person
From now on
I will write only
What I am feeling now
<u>Not</u> what I felt
Or what I will feel
Because where it will end
And where it began
And what time it is now
Would just get muddled up
And the traffic
Would start up again
And leave no room
For the weak
Or the sick
Or the poor
Even if
A chain is only as strong
As its weakest link
It is the traffic's duty
To take care
Of the weak
And the sick
And the poor
In the end
It makes us all stronger

#1512

After I Am Brave

I wait to see you
I wait to ask you
Your name
I wait to ask you
To go out with me
Then I see you
And we smile
And great each other
Then I see you again
And we shake hands
And politely introduce each other
After I am brave
I am politely turned down
And I turn and run away
Home to my four walls
Wondering if I should
Ever see you again
Wondering if I would
Ever see you again
Wondering if this shell
Of a life will be past
And I will find a connection
That will last

I remember a connection
And then I remember
Being bumped down a notch
And then I remember
You never seeing me
Miserable
After I am brave

#1513

Anymore Game

After I am turned down
Face down
Ass up
I end up
Not caring if I don't
See you again
You may oppose
The way I feel
Not wanting to play the game
Anymore
Sitting with people
Who don't care
If I live or die
Or people who
Would much rather see me
Never again
I go inward
And decide
After I am turned down
Again
Face down
Ass up
I end up
Not caring about anyone
Else but me
Myself
And I

#1514

Returns

I am a new book
That doesn't sell
And has a damaged cover
So the book store
Can't return me

You are all in perfect shape
And are getting sold
On a regular basis
So the book store
Is always ordering

#1515

Uh Oh

Complacency
When will you ever
Get better
Stagnancy
Never changing
Because of what has
Got you down
Are you alright?
Are you alright
Being in the same place
Thirty years from now?
Did you ever think
That the world you are making
Only has room for
You and your broken promises?
It doesn't make sense to me
Because you never tell me
If I can trust you
Where you are
And I just don't know why
It had to end like this
So what makes you act this way?
When it didn't have to be
Over like this

#1516

To Do Myself

I choose to sit by myself
Because I don't like your company
I choose not to play your game
Anymore
And even when I sit by myself
Someone invades my space
And I have to talk to them
To please them
When it makes me nauseous
To do so
I would rather eat razor blades
Than sit in a crowd
And have to lie by association
Lie by sitting with people
I don't like
Who don't like me
And play the game
I would rather
Not sell another piece of art
Than associate with you all
So
I choose to sit by myself
Whether it offends you or not
I would rather alienate myself
From you all
Than to sit with a crowd
That prefers incestuous inbreeding
To going solo
And experiencing something
Solely on their own
And growing with it
And seeing with their own eyes
And casting away all filters
To D.I.Y.

Not following group orders
To walk in a line
D.I.Y.
Not To walk in a line

#1517

Redeem

Sinners
Make the best
Lovers
I don't believe
In your god
Or any of your
Gods or devils
And you hold that
Against me
To this day
I am just as proud
To say
I am an Atheist
As you are
To say
You are a christian
In your god's eyes
We are all sinners
From the day
We are born
I cannot buy into
A spiteful god
That never gives
Anyone a chance
From day one
Twist this around
How ever you want
Sinners
Because I don't care
What you all think
Anymore
Sinners

#1518

I Am In The Dark

I write this
In pitch black darkness
These moments are precious
I never knew a gun
I knew rage
I never knew dealing death
I knew death
Those people who died
I was jealous of
The rich kids
And the popular kids
But not enough to take them away
From the world
Just jealous enough
To do something better
With my life
My family never pushed me
To deal death
But to make something
Of myself
As I write this
It hasn't happened
<u>Yet</u>
But I think that
I can see the light
At the end of the tunnel
Where as I think
You never could

#1519

Forgotten Or Mocked

I was just a kid
Laughing all the way
Down the highway
With friends
To see a band
Not realizing
That time is/was precious
Trying to forget
The bullshit of high school
A highway paved
By others just like me
Struggling not to lose
An uncertain future
Where the past
Would forgot or mock
My uncertain/certain future
I could have been you
But I wasn't
And I got by
Even though I was
Either forgotten or mocked

#1520

Golden Moment

I might as well have H.I.V.
For how you treat me
I never saw you again
I guess I never knew you
I could never get you down
From your high perch
So I leaned into the wind
And eventually caught a cab home
I never thought that this would happen
What did I know
You were dirty too
But I found out
The hard way
And now
Now
My calls are ignored
Well at least your Mom liked me
I am ready to go
Right now
Now
And now
Now
My messages
Are left unanswered
Well
At least your Mom liked me

#1521

A Painter's Indifference

I could ask you
Out
I could ask you
To be my friend
I could ask you
To be my girlfriend
My lover
My wife
But
I am not prime real estate
And I know this
And so do you
With how you treat me
It is pretty obvious
I am crying
For my hunger
For you
And your hair
Your skin
Your eyes
Your lips
Your breath
I am crying
For a house
That isn't inhabited
Anymore
I have been working so hard
To get out
Of my mess
And I am succeeding slowly
But to my despair
You never notice me
And my work

#1522

I don't have a B.A.
I don't have a P.H.D.
And I never will
Everything I have learned
Is from personal experience
Which saved me thousands of dollars
And I believe
Made me wiser
Than you and your teachers and professors

#1523

Bold Discretion

Is my message too bold?
Should I hide something?
Should I be more discreet?
More discreet with my feelings?
Should I chase you?

If my message is too bold
Too bad
If I hide something from you
I feel dishonest
Discretion is another word
For someone who should be feared
I am <u>not</u> to be feared
As for the chase...
If you make me run for you
Then you are not worthy of my time

I now know
What I must do...
Walk away
And cut my losses
By forgetting about you

#1524

Sad Songs

My eyelids become heavy
And my dreams push out
Putting my faith in a lottery
Putting my faith in you
When all it does
Is make me dizzy
And want to go home early
To listen to Lucinda Williams'
Sad songs that I just can't seem
To forget
But that's a good thing
When you are trying to learn
How to live
All I have left
Are the days ahead
I try to keep the faith
That the days ahead will be better
Than yesterday or today
I sleep so much now
My eyelids are shut tight
And my dreams are pushing out
While I sleep
With my sad songs
Playing away

#1525

Indifference

I am a stain
On your good dress
A stain
That makes you
Have to throw it out
The dress
Because no dry cleaner
Or stain remover
Can get me out
And now
You never want
To see me again
But what does it matter
Those clothes
Stopped fitting you
Months ago
When you lost
All that weight
So now
I am a stain
On a dress
That doesn't fit
That ended up
In a garbage bin
Out back of your
Apartment building
That some girl will
Pick out
And think
To herself
"That will do"
And walks away
With it dragging behind her
Happy enough

With her find
And me
And me
Still not happy
That I am still a stain
But happier less
Because I was
Passed over by you
And barely accepted
By a woman
Who is indifferent
With life
Indifferent
With her life
And indifferent
With me
Both seemingly
The same woman
And the same indifference
To me

#1526

The Last One

The earthworms
Are all on trial
This morning
And they have all
Just been found guilty
Forced out of their homes
By a three day non stop rain
They are all on the sidewalks
Crucified on the pavement
Left out to burn
On the first day of sun
Time is not on their side
Just like it is not
On mine
But I have said it before
That time is not on my side
And that I have to make something
Of myself
Before
I have a stroke
Before
I have a heart attack
Before
I go creatively impotent
And if these things all happen
Before I make something
Of myself
I will be on trial
Just like the earthworms
On trial
For a dirty past
Ignoring
My present
Ignoring

My future
That never comes to be
And next thing you know
I have been sentenced
And I have been
Sentenced to solitary confinement
For the rest of my life
And as for my death
It is meaningless
Just like
Billions of others

#1527

Horses And Hounds

Short term financial planning
At the tracks
Might as well buy a lottery ticket
And cross your fingers and toes
See them all
Running around on that track
And you hoping that
You too
Will finally get on the right track
And you can finally quit the grind
Leave your wife for the Caribbean
Or Barbados
Or someplace else
That is warm and has little or no taxes
Then you can blow it all
Again
On whiskey and lap dances
From women
Who don't care about your name
But do care about
That wad of fifties in your
Tight grip
And when it all runs out
Will you crawl back to your family
Hoping that they will take you back?
Or will you just jump off of the nearest
Cliff or bridge?
If you are only seeing
The short term
Then you will always miss
The long term

#1528

In And Out

Just breathe
In and out
And maybe
My voice will come back
But
Maybe
It never left me
I just wasn't looking
Hard enough
But
Maybe
I never had a voice
And after all of these years
I have yet to find one
Just breathe
In and out
And you will eventually
Get well
And you will eventually
Forget her
And her mean streak
I
Just
Have
To
Let it roll off of my back
Just breathe
In and out
I am now
Just breathing
In and out
And I have moved on
Thinking
That I just need a break

And maybe
I <u>will</u> find my voice
Again
But
I am starting to think
It never left me
I just need to
Breathe
In and out
And keep telling myself
Make myself better
And it will all work out
Just breathe
In and out

#1529

In Order For You

In order for you
To see me last night
I had to put out the lights
In order for you
To hear me this morning
I had to hang up the phone
But later on
I realized
That I can't wait
To see you again
My friends
My true friends
(You all know who you are)
Are closer than family
And if I don't show it
I am truly sorry
You all buy me dinner
And pop and tea and breakfast
And I feel like
I have nothing for you
But my loyalty
And honor
And honesty
And integrity
You all
The few I have
You all
Mean the world to me
And I hope
That this poem
Shows you
My gratitude
So take care
I just hope that

I am not too much
Of a bother to you
That you never forget me
Because I will never forget you
And I think about you all
All of the time
So take care
Please take care

#1530

Today

I don't feel inspired
But I don't feel tired
It is all a fraud
That is being broadcasted
That gets me down
Gets my hope up
Just to get knocked down
By a little game
All games are little
Because
I won't jump through hoops
For anyone
No one is worth being chased
All of the time
I am not a show dog
So I won't jump through
Your hoops
And when I see a friend
Jumping through hoops
Just to get a hug
Just to get in a new relationship
Just to get some tail
It
Just
Makes
Me
Sick
And then there is your girlfriend
Who ignores me most of the time
But with the occasional awkward smile
Or the more common looking away
I don't know what I did
To deserve all of that
But I guess it is not really important

Because I don't really like her
And then there is you
All young
And beautiful
And I think I creep you out
Just my luck
And then there is you
My age
And beautiful
And I think that I am not in your league
Just my luck
This all gets me down
And maybe
Just maybe
This is why
I don't feel inspired today
Oh well
There is always tomorrow
And hope for a better day

#1531

Disturbed Sleep

I worry about you
My young friend
About your
Cigarette smoking
Your drinking
And your choice
In "boys"
As you call men
I worry
That you will get
Stalked
Or beaten
Or taken away for good
And you will end up
Like many of my friends
Far away
With no more contact
I know that
I am very selfish
In my worry
Or at least
I think that I am selfish
Because I know that
You are one strong
Young lady
And if there are days
When the "boys" get you down
I know that it is tough
To get over
But
In the words
Of a washed up television star
It all means nothing
So wipe your ass with that

And move on
I truly hope
That you can move on
Because I know that
You have a good heart
And that you will eventually
Make some "boy" happy
And in turn
He will make you happy too

#1532

All At Once

The day I found out that
I didn't get the art show
I realized that
The three girls
I asked out
The three girls who said that
They would call me
Never did
And now it seems
They never will
Everyone says that
At least you tried
And
Nice try
But it is all of little consolation
These words of silence
These songs of illusions
These books and books
And books of sad solemn poetry
Someone said
Don't try
Just do it
So I carried my letters
Of rejection
To my bedroom
And add them to the pile
And I go to bed
And I try to sleep it off
Don't try
Just do it
More words
That were never
Heard
And never

Spoken
This is why
In the letter you wrote
I was glad
To finally hear from you
But now it is all
Just silence

#1533

Oblivious

I was on the bus
The other day
And I saw you
Coming home from work
You looked very sad
The young woman
Who was supposed to be
The one
The mother of my child
You were so deep
In your sadness
You were very nearly struck
By the bus I was on
I thought of the times
We had sex
And how your family thought
I was strange
For being an Atheist
And how much fun
We had at times
Oblivious
To all around us
My feeling now
Is that I am very lucky
To get out of that one way
Relationship
(Me to you)
By the skin of my teeth
I am just upset
That you seemed so happy
The last time
We were together
And that I was totally
Oblivious

To the crumbling foundation
And now
And now
I am the happy one
Moving on
And you are back
In your old ways
Before we met

#1534

Where Have All The Honest Women Gone?

Be prepared
For failure
For rejection
For oblivion
For excuses
For skin rubbed raw
For bleeding gums
For loneliness
For lies
For soft rejection lines
For humiliation
For one hundred years
More of this all

Here it comes again
The heat
The heat
Is stifling
I would rather hear
"Not interested"
Than hear
"Sure"
Or
"Maybe"
I have just one question to ask
"Where have all of
The honest women gone?"

#1535

Just The Facts

I take my glasses off
And rub my eyes
Vigorously
After seeing
Your naked image
I won't be going
To you again
I won't be pleasant
To you again
Just matter of factly
Just the facts ma'am
Just the facts
I put my glasses on
And walk away
From the facts
Just the facts
The cold hard facts

#1536

Little Consolation

I regret
Sharing that sunrise
With you
I regret
Sharing those fireworks
With you
I regret
Having sex
With you
I regret
Ever meeting up
With you

I guess
It is better
To regret
What you did
Than to regret
What you never did
Though
This is of
Little
Consolation
Right
Now

#1537

Days Of Ransom

Day 1:
I needed fifty dollars
In my bank account
Or else a cheque would bounce
I discussed this with
A "friend"
And he said
He would lend me the money
If I lent him
My three autographed
Skinny Puppy records
Which I have owned
For over twenty years
I already owed him ten dollars
Which I intended on paying
This "friend"
Back Friday
In seven days
I see it this way
This "friend"
Doesn't trust me
With his money
But expects me
To trust him with
Something that is irreplaceable
To top it all off
One of the autographers is dead
He gave me
No other choice
Money is replaceable
What I "lent" him
Is <u>not</u>
He also wants to "help me"
Get a new camera

So he has offered
To hold onto my money
Until I can afford
The camera of my choice
Now I know
What must be done
As soon as I get enough money
For rent and to pay
My "friend"
His sixty dollars
I will give him his money
Retrieve my records from him
And save the money
On my own
I will not speak to him
Until I have his sixty dollars
Whenever I think big
Something small happens
Whenever I think big
Something small happens?

Day 2:
Early in the morning
And I am thinking
About the S.N.F.U. song
"Devil's Voice"
And the last two lines
Of the song
"With each broken record
Died a part of me"
Incidently S.N.F.U. is the hostage taker's
Favorite band
Incidently my vinyl
Means everything to me
Along with
My books and cd's
And of course my work/art
At night

I start counting the hours
Until the phone calls start
Or at least
I hope that they start
Because the Taliban
Has stated that
"The hostages are still alive"
Whenever I think small
Nothing happens?
Whenever I think big
Something small happens?

Day 3:
9:16 in the morning
And the phone is silent
10:16 in the morning
And the phone is silent
11:16 in the morning
And the phone is silent
12:16 in the afternoon
And the phone is silent
1:16 in the afternoon
And the phone is silent
2:16 in the afternoon
The hostage taker called
To say that the hostages were fine
And that the deal is still on
3:16 in the afternoon
And the phone is silent
4:16 in the afternoon
And the phone is silent
5:16 in the afternoon
Two phone calls came
They were both concerned
With my predicament
But could not help
So they wished me well
6:16 in the evening

And the phone is silent
7:16 in the evening
And the phone is silent
At approximately 8:16
In the evening
I give up
And get into my bed
Without thinking
Big or small thoughts

Day 4:
In the middle of the night
An investor called
To say he may be able
To help me out
He asked what I had to offer
And I told him
And he said
He would get back to me
Later
The investor came through
Later
And I made the call
To let the Taliban know that
I had the ransom money
He will call me
To let me know
Where and when to meet him
And then reminded me
Not to get the authorities involved
I wait

Day 5:
Waiting for the call

Day 6:
Waiting for the call
I finally get the call

Come alone
With unmarked bills
Tomorrow
Is the day
Finally

Day 7:
I get the call
And I go meet the
Taliban representative
I pass him the money
And he releases the
Hostages
To my care
And they are relieved
(I am relieved too)
To be back in my home
But
Did I learn a lesson here
Never
Ever
Go to a loan shark
Or
I mean
A hostage taker
Or
I mean
A small "friend"
Because whenever I think
Small
Nothing happens
And whenever I think
Big
Small things happen
Either way
I just end up in trouble

#1538

The Dreams

The dreams
Of going to
The Territories and Alaska
Of two nights ago
Were replaced
By the dark brooding dreams
Of last night

Two nights ago
I met glorious peoples
Who loved their land
And wanted to stay
Canadian
No matter what
That Russian asshole
Says about or does at
The North Pole

Last night
I was in a dark arcade
Where young beautiful
Women
Gave their naked bodies away
For quarters
Or the occasional loonie
Or the even rarer twonie
This was <u>NOT</u> fun

My problems of yesterday
Dissolved in the water
Of territorial dreams
But my problems of today
Come back ten fold
When a beautiful

Young naked girl
Named "Christie"
Placated me
By saying that
I made her feel good

I would give up
The good
If the bad
Never reared their ugly heads
Again
Or at the very least
I
Could not
Would not
Remember the bad

#1539

And Now

I bleed
When I see
Your young eyes
And body
I bleed
When I hear
That you are fighting
With your boyfriend
I bleed even more
When I hear
About your and his
Reconciliation
And now
I bleed
When I write,
Think, see and hear
You

#1540

Charlie Kaufman

I watched a movie yesterday
It was about a man
Who fell in love with a woman
The woman eventually had the man
Erased from her mind
He was so distressed
He tried to have her
Erased from his mind
I wish I could
Erase my past 4 lovers
From my mind
The bad over shadowed
The good always
And 3 of the 4 lovers
I have never seen again
As for the other
I see her very very rarely
Even after my first girlfriend
I felt that I was dirty
And that I had been aged
By fifty years
In the movie
The man
Regretted getting her erased
And tried to stop it
So the movie over all was sad
But it had a happy ending
I feel like with myself
That there will never be
A happy ending with me
Maybe because I feel dirty
And fifty years older
Than I really am
And then I think about you

How I see you every weekend
I see your youth as being my ally
And then sometimes I see my age
As being your enemy
You have been seeing your current lover
For six years
And you tell me
That the two of you
Are always fighting
I don't think you realize
That this will age you
And I worry about you
And I think what good am I?
With my depression
And my pills
And my doctors
And my pot belly
And my music
And my books
And my paintings
And my photographs
And my writings
And my sense of humour
And now I think
Why shouldn't I deserve
A happy ending?
Why shouldn't I have
A happy ending?
The power of positive thinking eh?
Fucking rights!
I do deserve a happy ending!
We all do!

#1541

There's Always Losers

She said
Long time no see
She said
Good luck in life
I gave her my number
And she never called
To see me
I gave her my portfolio
And she never took
The initiative
To even ask to see me again
I write about you
I write about them
To get it out of my system
And still
It doesn't make me happy
There's always losers
There's always winners
In games
I know
I know they think
They are winners
And
I know
I know I am
The loser
You
She
They don't know
What it is like
Going to sleep
Every day
Feeling like this
One of the always losers

#1542

Taking Sides

There is a war inside me
And I am starting to take sides
You're never going to be safe again
You're never going to walk alone again
You're going to go to sleep
With the lights on all of the time
I am going to project
My xenophobia in your direction
I am going to project
My hatred at you some more
I am going to bring some violence
To the table
And get it tattooed on my face
You won't say it anymore
But I will say it lots more
It is called a funeral
For your weakness
I will wreck your life
And walk away
Without turning back
I took a side
That doesn't sing at all
And won't console you
After your life
Has been ruined
There is a war inside me
And I took a side
That got locked in my own prison
Inside

#1543

The Blacklisted

Let's get this done
I am the one who lies
Says I only smoke weed
When I do crack as well
I am the one who gets
An $118 ticket for
Smoking cigarettes in public
Because I am seventeen
I am old enough
To be her father
When I realize
That the thought
Of sex with her
Just pisses me off
Of sex with her
For money
Or crack
Or food
Or whatever
Just pisses me off
I realize that I am
$65 short on rent
And I don't even know
If she has a home
I would feed her
But like they say
You feed a stray once
And then it won't go away
And I feel guilty
For thinking this way
Let's get this done
And hope my guilt
Leaves me alone for once

#1544

6 To 7 Months

I met her a few weeks ago
Her name is Amanda
She always greeted me
When I went into the convenience store
She never asked for money
One day I was walking home
With a metric ton of camera equipment
And she offered to help me
It was a long hot day for me
So I said yes
And agreed to give her
Some money and food
We get to my apartment
And she had the most
Sheepish facial expression
As she thanked me for my money
I realized that I didn't have any food
Until the next day
She left

I see her again
A week later on pay day
And I buy her a juice
She tells me that
She is seventeen
And has to feed her weed addiction
I say
At least it is not heroin or meth
She agrees and thanks me and leaves
Seventeen
I wonder what would
Make a seventeen year old girl
Lose her grip on society or even life
Maybe it is because
I am old enough

To be her father
That she brings out
My parental side
I don't know

A week later
She asks me if I have a spare tooth brush
I offer her my bathroom
And she accepts
She does her thing
And thanks me and leaves
A week later
A friend and I
Are at the store getting slurpees
And Amanda comes from out of nowhere
With a 1967 Alex Colville silver dollar
In her hand
She is scratching her head and back
And everywhere in general
Which makes me think that
She is addicted to something
More than weed
She is this close
To begging us for five dollars
After we tell her that that is
What it is worth
But we have no more money
She sadly moves on
The next day she is fine
So I buy her a slurpee
And she scurries away

The next week
I try to buy again
She has Chef Boyardee
In a grocery bag
And she tells me a friend of her's
Calls himself

"Chef Boy R G"
When my bank card
Turns up empty
She buys
I feel awful
And tell her that
I owe her a meal
She waves at me
And says that
I don't owe her jack shit
Smiles are free
And that I have
Given her alot
Her smile melts my heart
And she tells me
That she won't stay
At the Youth Emergency Shelter
Because they just pity you
I am told this after I ask her
If she stays there
At that point she waves
And says goodbye
I worry that she
Has been raped
I worry that she
Is being raped
I worry that she
Will be raped

Now I can barely pay
My own bills
So I hope
That the next time I see her
She is doing OK
And none of the fucked up shit
That put her in
Her current position
Will come back

And make her
Give up
And give in
But I digress
It is not glamourous
To be seventeen years old
Six or seven months pregnant
And addicted to crack
And weed
And cigarettes
And the streets
It is just plain sad
Because she is killing herself
And her child
So all I can do
Is shrug my shoulders
And walk away
And pretend not to care
Or pity her

#1545

Pride

Pride
Is a strange beast
White pride
Black pride
Gay pride
Why be proud
Of something
You have no control over
Like skin colour
Or sexual orientation
I think that
There should be
A straight white person pride week
Oops!
But then I would be
Called a bigot
Don't be proud
To be a woman
Be proud to be a feminist
Don't be proud
To be a man
Be proud not to be sexist
Don't be proud
To be gay or bi
Be proud to be strong enough
To put up with the bigotry
You may face
Be proud
Of your work or art
Or your open mind
Don't close your mind
And be proud
Of something
That you have no control over

This sort of pride
Only starts borders
And raises walls
And I believe that
In life we were meant to
Tear down borders or walls
Not put them up

#1546

Laying Blame

He said
"Pretty big, eh?"
And
"At least I can look down
And see mine!"
And
"How do i spell relief?
P.I.S.S.!"
As he urinated on the
Freshly mowed lawn
There were four of them
Two boys
Two girls
All hopped up on something
Probably crack or meth
This is in broad daylight
2PM on a warm fall afternoon
While people are laying blame
People like me
Who have lived in this area
For decades
Get harassed by junkie pan handlers
Who simply say
"Give me some money."
I hold the bars responsible
I hold the business association responsible
So responsible
That I don't go out at night anymore
So responsible
That I remember back in 1995
I was attacked by two drunk boys
I didn't tell them
That I was a brown belt in Judo
And that I had been teaching

Judo for four to five years
I made short work of them
And then they decided
That they were going
To charge me with assault
Lucky for me
A few bystanders backed me up
If it wasn't for five or six stores
I would have moved years ago
But I feel that I am stuck here
With my current financial position
Stuck here with the
Junkie panhandlers and drunks
Stuck here writing about these losers
Worried about my safety
Worried about my work
Worried about my friends
All because
People are too busy laying blame
To see people like me
Are getting caught in the middle
Of a war that
Eventually
Someone will lose
And I worry that someone
Will be me
Or someone like me
That is
If it hasn't already happened
To someone like me

#1547

Shrug It Off

Tell me what you know
Don't just leave me
Out here to freeze
I think that my sadness
Overwhelms me
And those around me
Let's try and be friends
Tomorrow
As the sun is coming up
And as long as the sun
Keeps coming up for air
Maybe we can keep being friends
For as long as the sun
Keeps coming up for air
Even when
I don't feel like coming up for air
And if you have to leave me
Tell me what you know
Before you leave
Don't just leave me
Out here to freeze

#1548

Hypocritical Essays

When a woman says
She wants to cut off
A man's penis
She is praised
And when a man says
He wants to cut off
A woman's breast
He is scorned
And called sexist
How come a man
Gets called a stud
And is praised
When he fucks around
And a woman
Is called a slut
And is scorned
When she fucks around
How come a black man
Is considered cool
When he shaves his head
And when a white man
Shaves his head
He is a Nazi
I hope for
And look forward
To a day
When I can show my face
In public
And when these hypocrisies
Are thrown away
And are replaced
With an open mind
And an open heart

#1549

Sincerely Your's

I write this at work
To get started
I write this at work
To keep me going
I write this at work
To finish me off
I read this at work
To remind me of home
And what I have there
My books
My records
My cd's
My art
My fish
My bed
And you waiting
On the other end
Of the phone
So i write this all down
And read it to you
As a small reminder
To call me
And ask how my day was
And I will ask your day was too
Sincerely your's

#1550

3 Kittens At Sunrise

About the only thing
I miss about you
Is waking up in the morning
To see the sunrise
Together
One morning you had 3 kittens
And even though I am
Allergic to cats
They were so cute
Playing at the foot of the bed
While the sunrise
Gently spoke to all of us
I miss cuddling up
To your warm body as well
Then starting the day
On the right foot
Later on
When things went sour
And the cool fall air
Reminded me of us
I still woke early
Missing you
And missing how pure
We were
The cool fall air
Is when we met
And the bitter cold
Winter air
Is when we last saw each other
I often wonder
If the fall air reminds me
Of waking with you
What will the bitter cold
Winter air remind me of?

The darkness?

#1551

Missing For Good

Yesterday
I realized
That I hadn't seen you
In about a month
I now miss you
On my early morning walks
Miss you
When I get off of the bus
In the afternoon after work
I look for you
Up and down the avenue
I look for you
At the convenience store
Now I remember
Giving you my buzzer number
I wait for you
To buzz me
You never do
So
I look for you
At my front door
I look for you
Off of my balcony
And I realize
That with all of your troubles
Maybe you are missing
And that wherever you are
That slowly
Your problems
Are slowly being solved
And that maybe
Just maybe
You are missing
Missing for good

And that
Being missing
Is doing some good
I can only hope
That this is true
Because
It may ease the sting
Of missing you

#1552

Believe Me For Once

Behind
I want to love
What is behind the glamour
But you move
On a different plane
In and around the sky
And my roots
Are so deep
I am never able to fly
You don't believe me
When I tell you that
You don't need make up
You don't believe me
When I tell you that
I have a crush on you
You don't believe me
And now
I don't believe in myself
Because
You never hear me
When I cry out to you
And
You never hear me
Because you are busy
Flying away
And I am left alone
Looking at the sky
Hoping that I never see you again
Because
I try as hard as I can to fly
But my roots keep me here
Where I am safe
Never letting me stray
To a land of maybe hurt

Or a plane of maybe love
This sort of hurt
Makes me love my work
But it hurts my roots
Because
The more you go away
The more I wish that
I could go with you

#1553

Often

I think of you often

Having dinner with your lover
And having other indiscretions
Tight to the bone
Ever ready for your lover and children

My road gets weary without
You and your love

Love I miss dearly
In an increasingly dreary world
Fit for a loner
Easily wanting you after all of these years

Wanting some sort of contact
If it means just a letter
To let me know
How you are
Or how your parents, lover and children are
Underneath your hang ups
That burned me

You burned me
Often
Under the guise of love

#1554

Anybody But You

The cool fall air
Creeps into my room
Through the slightly opened window
And I can't help
But think of you
Blaming all of your irrational acts
On your illness
I promise myself that
I will never do the same
I will always take responsibility
For my actions
For all of my actions
Blaming your illness
Is like killing someone
While you are driving drunk
And then saying
It was the alcohol
That made you do it
No
You made you do it
This sadness
That envelopes me
Wishes for snow
Just a little snow
Because
Then the snow
Would be just a little closer
To melting
And that means
Life comes back soon
And that means
I can breath once more
And think about
Anybody but you

#1555

Prediction In Full

The lounge is full
Of people wearing armor
Waiting to be taken
Advantage of
Waiting
And waiting
Later on
I think to myself
That if you really
Wanted me
You would have called
I mean
I did give you my number
And all
I see how it will be
You will say
Long time no see
I've been busy with school
I've been busy with work
I am sick of half truths
I am tired of half lies
Why don't I ever hear
I've been busy
Fucking some rich
Physically fit career man
Or
I've been busy
Hanging around some guy
Who doesn't appreciate me
Oh, I know that you will treat me
Like a queen
But I would rather have
That arrogant self-centered boy
Who is mysterious

I don't want someone
Who will respect me
I want someone who will
Treat me like an unwanted
House guest
I would rather hear
That you think I am fat
Or you are not into
The starving artist routine
Than
I forgot to call you
I wouldn't say
I look forward
To our next meeting
I would say
I dread the time
When we meet again
For I will have to hear
Some more bullshit
About how busy you are
And you not caring
That this makes me feel
Like I am the only person
In the world
Who has free time on their hands
As I leave the armor lounge
I think to myself
What goes around
Comes around

#1556

Frowning Empty Moon

The empty moon
Frowns on me
Thus I am compelled
To provoke it to war
I paint, write and work
At night
When the moon says
I should be asleep
The moon's gaze stiffens
And I am off to the races
With my work
11:06 PM
12:10 AM
1:23 AM
Even 3:20 AM
I devise plans
To overthrow
The moon's politics of time
And strike at its heart
The moon
(Full or partial)
Bleeds onto my work
And I create more work
Until I get a migraine
From lack of sleep
And the moon is bled empty
Weak enough
That even a small vision
Of the sunrise
Crushes the moon's shell
And I am left happy
That I have worked enough
That I crushed something
Other than my

Family and enemies and my faults
The moon has never been part
Of my family
The moon has always been
An enemy
That shines on my faults
Now in this darkness
I shine on the moon like a flare
A shiny fist lunging
For the moon's gaze
And for once
I am a winner
Of this war
With the frowning, empty moon

#1557

Bar Hopping

Sitting in a bar
Drinking drinks
Going to another bar
Bar hopping
Till you're drunk
Into oblivion
Guess what?
Killing your central nervous system
Is <u>NOT</u> cool
No matter what you think
No matter what you wear
No matter what you drink
No matter who you are with
No matter who you meet
I outgrew that bullshit
Fifteen years ago
And now
Most weekends
I stay home
Because it is just not safe
To go out
And run into a drunk
Coke head
Who thinks that they are bulletproof
They are foolish loose cannons
You never know
What they will do
So if one of them ends up dead
I won't shed a tear
Because they are <u>NOT</u> worth it
So I sing this song for you
The sober home loner on the weekend

#1558

Intruder

I think he knows you are here
I think he knows I am here
I think to myself that
"I may not get out of here alive"
And I hustle out the back door
Pulling up my pants quickly
Doing my shoelaces and belt
In a few quick motions
I get outside to the
Cool fall air
Where I can see my breath
And catch the first bus
Out of Dodge
Hopefully he didn't know anything
Hopefully he doesn't know anything
And what he doesn't know
Won't hurt him
Because it was just
A deep conversation
One he never has with her
And I think to myself
"Will I ever get a chance?
And if so
Will I make the most of it?"
All of this comes to me like
The tides on a hot summer day
And that's when I realize
It is fall
Not summer
And everyone besides me
Thinks that talk is cheap
I stretch out in my seat
On the bus
And try to get some sleep

With this gloomy thought
Stumbling around in my head
What a day!

#1559

Another Beginning

I read your worried love poems
About your latest lover
Ever since I met you
It starts the same way
And usually ends the same way
All hot and passionate
At the start
And then
All hot with anger and disappointment
At the end
There is a pattern here
Like a carefully knit sweater
That starts out as a ball of wool
And ends up with an article of clothing
A child's sweater
That is worn for a year or two
And then donated
As a hand-me-down
To a younger sibling
Or donated to the Goodwill
Or the Salvation Army
Or Value Village
Because it holds memories
That are all fuzzy
Then someone else
Gets the sweater
More fuzzy memories
And discarded again
For someone else
To use and then discard
This piece of written work
Is just one person's perception
Of the joy you go through
Then

Of the worried pleasure
You go through
Then
The bitter sting
Of angry disappointment
Take what I say
With a grain of salt
Because
Even though I am 12 years
Your senior
I have little experience
In your vocation
So my written word
Cannot be fully trusted
I will just stand back
And watch the action movie
Until it ends
And
Then
Shrug my shoulders
And walk away
Feeling helpless
And somehow
For some reason
Incomplete
Again

#1560

Respectfully Your's

This blue eyed boy
Is tired of life again
Tired of all the doors
Slamming shut in his face
Tired of seeing people
Who don't care
Whether he lives or dies
It is a trouble
When another person
Is ignorant
For no other reason
Than they have more power
Than he does
Sometimes
This blue eyed boy
Dreams of fortune
And with it
The opportunity
To hide more often
Than without fortune
He sees his stack of books
Waiting to be printed
Piling higher and higher
And it just gets to him
Gets to him
Gets him sadder than before
Thinking to himself
"This blue eyed boy
Is tired of life again,
What will it take
For the tables to turn?"
And him finally
Respecting himself
As well as

Finally getting respect
From others

#1561

Boy In A Coma

You treat me
As if I have been in a coma
For years
Checking up on me
Once a year
To see if I am still alive
Because you may feel guilty
If I woke up
And asked if you stopped by
So you come by
And see me sleeping
(Weather permitting of course)
And then leave
Forgetting about me
For another year
What does it matter
I won't know the difference?

#1562

Might As Well

Don't leave me out here
Don't lock me outside
I swear that I did nothing
Wrong
Don't put me up here
You are the one
With major issues
I am the one
Who is just plain sad
Because your major issues
Are absorbing me
And tearing me up
To the point
Of no attachment

A half an hour later
I am shivering
From the cold
Still outside
Hoping that you will relent
Realizing
That you will not help me
I walk away
Knowing full well
That there is no point
In stalking anyone
Because when they don't
Want and/or need you
You might as well be dead

#1563

Accidents Will Happen

Because of accidents
You alienate me
From others
And make me
Hate my life
And hate myself
You are so young
And beautiful
You make me ache
To be so much
Older than you
The pain inside me
Grows every day
That I breathe
Grows to pain me
In ways
School never did
And yet
I still feel as if
I am in school
Because I am still
Learning new ways
To despise
What I have grown
Accustomed to
Lack of money
Lack of love
Lack of stability
Money, love and stability
Is what I now ache for
And because of accidents
I am getting used to this ache

#1564

So Sorry

So sorry
I couldn't breathe more
Around you
Early on
You took my breath away
And never gave it back
You couldn't
Or wouldn't
Care enough about me
That you couldn't
Or wouldn't
Return my love
To me

So sorry
That we had to part ways
But why should I apologize
You
Left
Me
No you will never know
How much I cared about you
And how lost
I feel
Without you
If this is the case
Then shouldn't you apologize to me?

#1565

First Snowfall

The snow gently lands
On the ground
For the first time
Of the season
The snow gently lands
On the ground
Like a baby's eyelids closing
Eyelashes coming together
And the baby
Goes to sleep
Just like all of the grass
And leave-less trees
They go to sleep
For another year
And I wonder
If the snow will stay
Or if the sun will
Melt it away
So I will have to wait
For another set of eyelashes
To close
And for it to happen all over
Again
Not that I mind really
No matter my mood
The first snowfall
Always moves me
To believe in softer things
In the world around me

#1566

Crash

Pacing around
Like a caged animal
Breathing hard
Thinking about your beauty
Knowing full well
I could be your Dad
Should be
Would be
Could be worse
It could be my birthday
Next week
Oh yeah
It is my birthday next week
It is no use
We are all getting older
And I am starting to care
Less
Don't do this
Don't do that
Fuck you
As long as I am
Not hurting anyone
What do you care?
What does anyone care?
I see you sitting alone
Wanting desperately
For you to ask me over
But I know you won't
Because you're like all of the
Others
You don't have the balls
So I continue pacing
My breathing gets easier
And I am starting to relax

Now knowing full well
No one is worth it
Worth the stress
Of it going wrong
You know
I am starting to get used to
This solitary life
There seems to be
Less stress this way
Nothing is worth stressing
And obsessing over
Unless it is your art
And your art should be perfect
Air tight and seamless
Just get it out
Drop it down
And watch it go off
Not caring what anyone thinks
Except yourself
And back onto
The subject of you
Goodbye.

#1567

Fear

I am not getting paid
By you
To please you
And even if I was
Getting paid
By you
I still wouldn't worry
About pleasing you
It is not my job
To please you
It is my career
To please myself
It is my career
To provoke you
Out of your pop culture
Stupor
I have no time for you
The process of weeding out
I don't need spring
As an excuse
To drop a few stragglers
From my book of lists
It is now my career
Even if I don't make a cent
It is my career
To destroy your image of me
And recreate myself
And do it all over again
Until I get the biggest smile
On my face
Knowing that my career
In life is
To provoke
And please myself

I do it for myself
And I will continue
Until my heart
Stops beating
And my lungs
Stop breathing

#1568

Not Sitting With You

I am not playing
This game anymore
I don't like your work
I don't like your talk
And I don't like you
I don't want
To get inside
Your hollow head
I would rather
Be with the other outcasts
Who appreciate me
And my work
And I know that they are
Few and far between
But I am far more comfortable
Out on the fringes
Than
In with the "in crowd"
Any day of the week

#1569

Four

These things
I can't forget
Playing Pool at 5 AM
Then going for breakfast
Then going home
And talking for hours
About everything
And nothing
Then going to bed
And sleeping
The trouble away

These things
I can't forget
Helping you
With your
Grade 9 level of English
Then telling me
After we had sex
That you had a boyfriend
Who packs a gun
Then ditching me
In Vancouver

These things
I can't forget
Me showing you around
This city of mine
Then going for martinis
And after the alcohol
Going back to my place
And you saying
"It looked like I needed a kiss"
Then everything going sour

And never seeing you again

These things
I can't forget
Meeting for the first time
And then not long after
Everything getting all hot
And passionate
And then you getting pregnant
And then you having an amniotic pregnancy
Blaming it on me
And after Valentine's Day
I never saw you again

These things
I can't forget
Wishing I was
Still a virgin
Realizing that
I have never bled so much
Forcing me to try
To forget your faces
Your touch
And everything else
That came with you

Unfortunately
These things
I will never forget

#1570

No One Is Coming Over

Sometimes
I feel like
My heart is a target
And my head is the sniper

She is only twenty one
And has been seeing
Her current boyfriend
For six years
And from what she has told me
They have been fighting
For five of those six years
I suggest counselling
Because they are
Practically married
She tells me that
He won't go
And that she thinks
About hurting herself
All of the time
I tell her that
I have been there
And show her
A few of my scars
For proof
Then I tell her that
It is not worth it
And that
A lot of people
Would be upset
There are so many other things
I would like to tell her
I should tell her
I could tell her

But my emotions
Get the better of me
Maybe I am only saying this
Because I have a crush on her
Because my heart is a target
And that my head is the sniper
I realize that
No one is coming over
And I also realize that
I am OK with this fact
Because the suns sets
Because the tide goes out
And eventually
The sun will rise again
The tide will come in again
For there has to be hope
For there is always tomorrow
A new day
A new start
A new challenge
I just hope that my young friend
Realizes this sooner
Rather than later
Realizes this sooner
Before her emotions get the best of her
And they take her down a path
That she can't return from

Sometimes
I feel like
My heart is a sniper
And my head is the target

#1571

Be Positive That You Are Honest

If you go in
Thinking that
You may get hurt
Then
You <u>will</u> get hurt
If you go in
Thinking that
This may be the one
Then maybe it will be
The one
And if it isn't
Then maybe it will
Happen again
And work out
The next time
There are many fish
In this sea
If everyone you see
Ends up hurting you
Then maybe
<u>You</u> have the problem
<u>Not</u> them
I am tired
Of people who are negative
About the sex
That they are interested in
And I have decided
To weed these people
Out of my life for good
If you get a broken heart
So what?!
It happens to everyone
Deal with it
And move on

And be positive
That you are honest
With yourself
Because everything works out
In the end
And it is always
For the better
As time always shows
Things always work out
For the better

#1572

Much Return

I keep on giving
I keep on taking
And nothing comes back
Maybe a little comes
My friends
My true friends
Treat me well
And sometimes
I feel as if
I don't return much
I feel like
I should be doing more
And then I get low
And lower
And lower
I keep on thinking
That some day
My ship will come in
And I can finally treat
My short list of friends
And hope that
It is as much in return
As they have given me

#1573

That Bird Has A Shadow

That one bird
Has a shadow
Which is unusual
These days
Because the rest of
The hens sound the same
She blasts her words
Out of a cannon
You all sound breathy
And like you are going
To have an orgasm
With every syllable
Do you all even realize
How ridiculous you all sound?
She is so far above you all
That you all and all your words
Are six feet under
And that bird
Is way up on a pedestal
Or a stage
You all will always be small
You all will always sound the same
And she will always
Stand out from the crowd
Using a huge sound system
Casting a large shadow
While you all speak
Under your breath
Hidden in her shadow
With limited style
And no substance
Always to be dwarfed
By her large style and
Even larger substance

#1574

You Are A Small Man

You wouldn't say it
To her face
So don't say it
Behind her back
You are a small man
Who thinks only
Of your pocket book first
And of what is between your legs second
You are a small man
I once was a small boy
Then I grew up
And chose to honor my partner
Treat her like a queen
And if I felt
I couldn't
Wouldn't
Shouldn't
Say it to her face
I couldn't
Wouldn't
Shouldn't
Say it behind her back
I care about money
But not over a human
A friend
Or a lover
You are a small man
So small
I never missed you
Once you were out
Of my life

#1575

You Are A Small Man: Part 2

Criticizing someone
Behind their back
Writing about women
Only as sex objects
Both are easy to do
When
The subject you are criticizing
Someone over
You yourself
Have never accomplished
It is called jealousy
And it is as green
As the money in your wallet
Writing about women
Only as sex objects
Disgusts me
To the point
Where I want to take
The pen I hold in my hand
And stab it in your neck
You come off
As a sexually frustrated
Jealous old man
And I hope
That when we next meet
I can be the better man
And bite my tongue
Instead of your balding head

#1576

Discipline

It is a half moon
When I decide
To do what I can do
To not fall in line
One desire
To be with you
Even though
You said "No"
And I already
Had you wrapped up
In a dream
Right up to where
You said ever so kindly
That you had a boyfriend
All these years
Am I myself?
All these questions
All these broken vows
All these friends
Who are run ragged
Take control
Because it takes discipline
To get through this life
Because the past bleeds
Because the present is a blood clot
And the future is for
Taking control
It is a half moon
When I decide
To do what I can do
To make myself happy first
And to please you second
I think that I understand now
I can't move on

Until I try again
And again
And again
Until I get it right
And eventually
I will get it right
With discipline
I <u>will</u> get it right

#1577

On Me Or Two

This time last year
We were sleeping together
After watching
The New Year's fireworks
After having sex
Now it is all over
And do you want to know
What I learned?
That all religions
Can lick my asshole
She and her family were
Christians and believed in god
And they had so many hang ups
Now I know
Everyone has a hang up
Or two
But don't take them out
On me
Now I am listening to
Slayer's latest album
And thinking about
That German girl at work
Who he said that
She was "intellectually tasty"
I told him
To give me a good referral
And now I hope
That if she isn't an Atheist
That she is at least Agnostic
And that she doesn't do drugs
And smoke
And drink
Er...um...
I guess

I am picky
But at least
I am not a delusional
Religious person
I will wake up for work
And hope for a new day
Where christians
Won't ram their shit
Down my throat
Because
As one put it
"God is for everyone"
I will say it one more time
Because you religious assholes
Didn't seem to listen to me
The first time
All religions and religious people
Can lick my asshole

Except for my Grandmother
And my Buddhist friends
Because there is always
An exception to every rule
And just remember what
The mighty Crass said in 1979
"Jesus died for his own sins
Not mine."

Happy New Year religious fuckheads
Happy New Year

this piece was written at 7:04 AM
on January 1, 2008
in Edmonton

#1578

His Heart

What can I say?
He taught me so much
And his kindness
Washed over me
Like an Ocean's tides
His sense of humour
Always made me smile

What else can I say?
He will continue teaching me
And being kind to me
And he will continue
To make me laugh
Because his heart is just too big
To stop beating this early on in his life

Thanks for still being there friend

this piece was written
on January 15, 2008
in Edmonton

dedicated to Mike Gravel

#1579

Now I Say

"I bet you hate my guts
Because I never called you back?"
"I've been busy."
She nods gravely
I told her it was becoming
A pattern
And that I didn't want to
Deal with it anymore
Serves me right
For trying to befriend
A 24 year old girl
So immature
So immature
We are all busy
But at least I make an effort
To call my friends
To keep in touch
One: You criticized me on your blog
Two: You stood me up three times
Three: You never return my calls
You are just like all of the
Immature young girls I know
So now I say goodbye
And I truly believe that
I am better off
Without you around

#1580

You Are All So Typical

Typical christian
Avoid anything that questions
Your religious beliefs

Typical christian woman
Gets defensive and angry when
Someone questions
Your religious beliefs
And you get condescending
When confronted by anyone
Different

Typical 35 year old divorced christian woman
Gets angry when
Someone points out your hang ups
That caused your relationship
To fall through
And not wanting to admit
You are a cliche
Who won't revisit anything
Because you are just plain lazy

Typical 35 year old divorced christian single woman
Afraid of people
Who disagree with your
Way of telling your children
What to believe in
So that it must be something
Because to believe in nothing
To believe in no religion
Or no anti-religion
Goes against your grain
And you can't have children
Who are different from you

You say we have some things in common
I seriously hope not
Because you are all a cliche
And are all so typical
So typical
You think that you are open minded
But you have proved to me

That you are not
Because if you are open minded
I would rather be the opposite to you
You are a lazy narrow minded cliche
You are so typical
Oh so typical

#1581

Don't Call Me

Don't call me
Bud, chum,
Pal, buddy,
Friend, acquaintance,
Lover, brother,
Son, Boy
Or even kid, kiddo
It is time to sour
With no regrets
No remorse
No love
No hate
Because I took the blame
So you now say
We are good friends
Well,
I owe you nothing
Except my back
As I am walking away
You don't find the time
So now I don't either
Because you
Don't call me
We were lovers
But now you
Don't call me
This is a handbook
On alienation
When you
Don't call me
I just hope that
In ten years
You think
Time heals all wounds

Because it doesn't in this case
So
Don't call me

#1582

Contrary To Popular Belief

I see nothing wrong
With hatred
Hatred of religions
Where a woman
Is forced to cover herself
From head to toe
Hatred of religions
Where homosexuality is a sin
Divorce is a sin
Birth control is a sin
Hatred of people
Who think christianity
Is an "alternative"
When it is really the status quo
Hatred of people
Who exude fake kindness towards me
And who believe
I am a lost soul
Who needs to be saved

Contrary to popular belief

I do not hate people
Who do not like
My hair
My tattoos
My clothes
My work/art
My taste in music
My Atheism
My mental disorder
My filthy mouth
And my even filthier mind
My personal politics

And my heroes
Or the way I keep
My cards
Close to my chest
Or my way of being quiet
When I should be loud
And vice versa

Contrary to popular belief

I have only a few friends
And I will keep it that way
Because I don't like crowds
I love my close family
Because they are the only
One I have
And I have the utmost respect for
My friends and family
I may not show it
But it is there
Trust me
I am proud of my talents
And I love all of my work
And I put everything
Into my work
Because along with my work
My family and my friends
They all get me through the night
Because their kindness is strong and true

One could say
My hatred's and my love's
Aim is true
Because they both
Have direction
And contrary to popular belief
Without you or your religions
Or your stale diatribes

I have direction
My love guides me
And is fuel for my work
My hatred sometimes
Puts blinders on me
And I cannot rest
Until I use it as fuel too
I am happy with my life
As a pig in shit
And just as content too
Contrary to popular belief

Contrary to popular belief

#1583

Cancer And A.I.D.S.

If I was a doctor
I would be
A mad scientist
I know I would
Get up every day
Angry that I still hadn't
Found the cure
To Cancer
Or A.I.D.S.
I know that I am not
Responsible
For the creation
Of these diseases
But I would feel
Responsible
With every passing
Death
With every passing
Second
That I did not solve
These mysteries
Yes
I would make
A good
Mad scientist
But somehow
I am glad I am not
The furious scientist
Because
I don't want
All of that responsibility
Heaped on me
For I would
Go mad

And be an angry doctor
A mad scientist

#1584

This is my response to a few Americans who criticized me on the internet. To protect the ignorant, the female shall be called "Hosehead" & the male shall be called "Hoser".

I just thought that I would take time between my two jobs to send Hoser and Hosehead a response, even though one of you implies my mouth is open too much and the other complains about my silence. Oh well, you can't please everybody.

1: Hosehead not wanting to "re-hash old entries" is sheer laziness because i see nothing wrong with sending me the links to appropriate pages with information that could possibly change my mind. I do it all the time.

2: As for me mocking Hosehead, yes I did, only after she called me a pet name MOCKINGLY. The only people who can call me pet names are my parents, my grand parents and my current girlfriend. Hosehead is (thankfully) none of the above.

3: Hoser had you read the rest of my "silly hat rant" (see poem #1596 on page # 411 of this book you are now holding) you would have read that I do NOT believe in any prophets, messiahs, gods, devils, heavens or hells. To quote Hosehead, "you should have done your homework."

4: I deleted Hosehead's response to my critique of her because it did not offer any insight to my brilliant writing skills. By the way, I delete far more comments than I let be posted and most of the time the people who I graciously let their comments grace my blog with their comments are ones I know personally. As for you two, well, need I say more.

5: Hoser called me a coward yet he is the one who hides behind a N.R.A. card and a gun. Anybody who hides behind a gun is a coward, I have been teaching Judo for 10 years and I still don't feel the need for a gun. Oh Hoser, what's this fascination with guns? I think you must be over-compensating for a small penis or something of that nature.

6: I respect myself first and foremost and I believe that no self respecting human being should want and/or need pity, in other words if you pity anyone it should be your sorry excuse for an insult. I started off by saying that I took this time between my two jobs to respond, my first job being practicing and the teaching of neurosurgery at one of the hospitals in this city and my second job at night is an air traffic controller at the international airport. So a few days ago three colleagues and I were discussing your sorry ass attempt at a blog and I said that Hoser called my tattoos "derivative", my three colleagues asked in unison (the same thing I asked myself), "derivative of what?" I see that you are a graphic designer for television so I understand it might be hard to grasp the english language when you are drawing and looking at pictures all day. I will help you out, there is a book called a <u>dictionary</u>. In this book it has definitions of all words in the english language, for your ease I will now place a link to a website called dictionary which has a definition of "derivative". I would suggest that before you use big words you try a dictionary first. Once you have mastered that book you may want to graduate to something called a "thesaurus", and no it is not a large, extinct reptile. It is another book, feel free to look up "thesaurus" in a dictionary if you would like. If you were trying to insult me and my lifestyle choice for body art I would suggest a smaller word, like "dumb" (the "b" on the end is silent) I think it is safe to say you know what "dumb" means because when referring to people like you "dumb" is usually followed by "ass", which is what my American brother calls Americans (the likes of which he is embarrassed by) who fall into several stereotypes. **1:** Americans who can't read **2:** Right wing Americans who can't read **3:** Religious right wing gun-toting wing nut Americans who can't read. So to keep a level playing field I will stereotype myself as well.

So up here in Canada in our muk luks and snow

shoes all we do is hunt moose, watch hockey and drink beer, eh. We don't know anything about you savages...er...Americans and your guns and we are all far too busy building igloos and breeding dogs to run our sleds. So if you don't like some or all of this rant, what are you going to do, declare war on Canada, invade us and shoot us all? My final parting words...
Take off, eh!

#1585

Dusty Halls

I'm the one
To start my own religion
In the dusty halls
Of big old buildings
I don't need
Any martyrs
I don't need
Any symbols
I don't need
Any drugs
The only books
I need
Are the ones
That speak of
Alienation and solipsism
The occasional friend
Is needed
To keep me grounded
But they don't need
To make any donations
Of monetary value
Just the knowledge
That they are there
When called upon
I am the one
Who can call my own
Shots
As long as I have
Respect
For myself
And for the people
I keep close
In these dusty halls
Of this old building

I will get by
Just fine
For
I am the one

#1586

In A Subway Station

You said that
You lost your virginity
In a subway station
I wonder
What is more traumatic
Losing your virginity
Or
Getting attacked
And beaten up
In a subway station
You could use both
As sign posts
I see no romance
In a subway station
And I see no safety
In a subway station either
I see you and your
Skinny body
Getting snapped like twigs
Or getting turned on
In a subway station
I fear for you
The same way
I fear for myself
Put a camera
In every nook and cranny
And I will still not feel safe
Mop the floors
Until you can eat off of them
And I will still not feel safe
No matter how warm
I would rather walk
And leave the safety concerns
To you

You are so young
And every time I see you
Go into a subway station
I will worry
About another
Sign post popping up
I will keep my trap shut
And avoid the subways
And take the buses
Leaving you with your secrets
That you can't ignore
And leaving me with concerns
That I can't ignore
I get off of the bus
And do up my jacket
Nice and tight
Feeling safe in the cold
Where the blanket of safety
Will wrap me up
Easier than if I was underground
Where the trouble starts
And where your indiscretions occur
I realize that I worry
Over nothing
Because nothing is exactly
What you worry about
Down there in the warmth
Of another sign post
We go our separate ways
And that is how it always ends
Between us
You said that
And I feel that
Agree to disagree
Disagree to agree
And go our separate ways
Because what you say
Is just a good way

To keep people at a distance
So you can go underground
And never see the light again
And I will stay up
Where the light is
Knowing that eventually
I will find someone
Who won't make excuses
For <u>not</u> getting close to people
And will actually
Want to get close
Instead of constantly
Pushing away
Down away
Into underground

#1587

The Eyes Have It

I couldn't help it
But to look at your eyes
The blues
Staring back at me
Open
But not all of the way
Just like your mouth
Saying things
I really needed to hear
And realizing
That I may have
Met my match
In heart size
I am not saying
We should
Fall in love
Get married
Have children
Retire together
And then grow old together
You just don't know
How beautiful it is
To meet someone
I get along with
At this point in my life
I listen to your words
And hear your music
And I realize
I want to listen
And hear more from you
And I just hope that
You feel the same way I do

#1588

Dreams Of Me

Dreaming of me
With you
In your car
I am driving
And I drop you off
At the base of a mountain
And you go into
This industrial warehouse
With eyes all big and brown
I take off
On a joy ride
And damage your car
In the process
I get scared
Because I know
I will see your
Big brown eyes
Go black with rage
Because I was so
Irresponsible
Because I am so
Irresponsible
Because I will be so
Irresponsible
And then
I wake up
All scared
Because I ruined your car
And that you are still
Here
With me
Where I will feel
Your rage
Dreaming of you

And your rage
But waking up
Just before I feel
I feel your wrath
I know
I know that these are just dreams
But I just can't help
Wishing that you were here
With me
As my back up protector
From the dreams of me

#1589

Losing Light From

The losers
Are paying
For the winners
To win
The losers
Keep on sinning
And the winners
Keep on winning
And sinning
And I am in the middle
Never winning much
Never losing much
Never sinning
In my eyes anyways
In my eyes
I am waiting
For my first breath
Of light from you
The excuses are there
And my open heart
Is here
Waiting to finally win
But maybe
Just maybe
I don't need you to win
And maybe
Just maybe
When I do win
There will still be
A vacancy of loss
That you never even tried
To fill

#1590

Fuck Unions

Alright now
All right now
Are we all right now?
Buying our way
Into others' hearts
And then coming back
A week later
For a full refund
You get away scott free
While the seller
Has a nervous breakdown
When they are laid off
You the buyer
Owe us a living
And respect
Not some government
Union prick who doesn't care
Take your union
And stuff it
In your fat union ass
Your new talk
Are the same old lies
That don't fix
Anything
I lied
I won't vote for you
I will eventually
Get what I want
From you
And when I do
Here
Will start the revolution

#1591

I Don't Think They Know

Gradually
I am accepting
My illness
Partly because
My good friends
Have accepted me
As is
And this helps me
Through the dark times
The other part to this
Is that
Out of anybody
In this small world
<u>YOU</u> are the one
That can do the most
Good or damage
To yourself
By yourself
One lie
By yourself
To yourself
You might as well
Get shot
In a drive by
I truly believe this
And this is helping me
To get through
The dark times as well
So that when you are bright
You can share it
With everyone around you
Be it family, friends or even enemies
There is a calm
About me now

When I am alone
That I am more
Comfortable with myself
More than ever before

#1592

There Are No Little Lies

The people
Who lie about the other persons
Do more damage
To themselves
Than to the other persons
That they lie about

If you
Lie to yourself
You are doing more damage
To yourself
And your family and friends
Than to the other persons

#1593

I Don't Like That Pair

I was asked why
I did not go to
His book launch
I put it simply that
I do not like his writing
Or his girlfriend's writing
They are both
Stuck in junior high school
With their writing
And the way
They act around each other
His rat a tat tat
Vocals
To her breathy slow
Vocals
(Which by the way
Is just like
Most of the women
Who come here)
Annoy me to no end
Come back to me
Get back to me
In 10 years
And if you have not progressed
In those 10 years
Then
You will never progress
And staying the same
Is just as bad
If not worse
As falling in reverse
So if I fall asleep
While they are reading
Wake me up when

That pair are finished
So I can get to bed
At a good hour
And forget that pair
By the next sunrise

#1594

Marginally Better

One night
I read a piece
About my love
For my good friend
Steve, my Japanese/Canadian Judo instructor
It was about
How much
He had been through
Like he had been interned in a P.O.W. camp
Even though World War 2
Was overseas
Even though he was born in Canada
Along with his parents
His parents did not agree with
What Emperor Hirohito
Was doing
I.E. starting a war
From what I gather
Only the military seemed
To agree with Hirohito
And that was probably because
They were brainwashed

The next night
You read a piece
Damning all Japanese
Because of what the
Brutal Japanese military did
To your Grandfather
Again, the military did it
Because they seemed to be brainwashed
The Japanese civilians and
Japanese/Canadians were not
You bigot

You read all breathy like every other woman
It sounded as if you were going to come
With every syllable
I have to say
You work is better than woman #1176
But not as good as woman #498
At a contest you won
You stared at me in triumph
Your win says just one thing

You are totally bland and palpable
No juries
No prizes bitch
I have no doubt that
You will go far
Because of your mediocrity
But you won't see me
Buying any of your shit
Throwing in an odd
Sexual encounter
Or bitching about the weather
Or laughing just to laugh
Or
Blah
Blah
The next time I see you
I will have already
Forgotten your name and your work
Because it is just not worth wasting
The brain capacity on such mediocrity

#1595

The Sky

Think of an ocean
With a calm blue sky
And think of a middle aged woman
Reading simpleton poetry
Only about
Calm blue skies and oceans
And reading well over the time limit too
Reading as if
As if
She is going to have an orgasm
After every line

She is wanting so badly
To be like everyone else
That she forgets herself
I have to ask, why be like everyone else?
It has been done before
Now think of this all
Being done
By thousands upon thousands of women
So called "poets" everywhere
In the whole fucking
Blue sky world

#1596

Silly Hat

A few years ago
One of my Aunts
Gave me a toque
For Christmas
It is black
With red devil horns
The responses have been mixed
Once when I was wearing it
One woman called me
"Satan's helper" and an "infidel"
I have to say that
If your faith is that put off
By a silly hat
Then obviously your faith
Is not very strong
By the way, just for your information
I do <u>NOT</u> believe in any
Prophets, messiahs, gods, devils,
Heavens or hells
And I am quite comfortable
With my life
So, to quote Hank Williams Sr.
"Mind your own business"
Because it is just a silly hat

#1597

Ignorance And Gluttony

I have been working
At a call centre for pizza
For almost three years
And people's lack of respect
Is unbelievable at times
Today
Some guy calls in
And his pizza is three minutes late
And he is all angry
And demanding a credit
I think
That if three minutes
Is your biggest worry
Then you have a pretty easy life
Which is what I think
Most westerners do
We have it so easy
Hey buddy!
Did you know
That some places don't have
Food or water
Let alone delivery of food?
Most of the people
I talk to on the phone
Piss me off
And make me feel so dirty
That I have to have a shower
Immediately when I arrive home
If it wasn't for
The flexible hours
Reasonable pay
And the nice people to work for and with
I would have been gone
A long time ago

#1598

Early Spring?

It is the middle of February
And the weather has been
Unseasonably warm
Snow is melting
Birds are chirping
Spring is my second favorite
Time of year
(Fall is the first
Because of the warm colours
In the trees and sun
And you feel change is in the air
Just like in spring, change is in the air)
Usually at this time of year
The temperatures are around
Minus 30, not plus 10
I will not take this for granted
And I will go out
As much as possible
And enjoy it all
Because
Even though it is still
The middle of February
I believe it is a sign
Of good things to come
Snow melting
Birds chirping
First lawn mower mowing
And then summer
You must enjoy it while it lasts
Because
You know what they say
About the weather on the prairies,
If you don't like it
Then wait a minute

#1599

To You

Late at night
I get a call from you
And you let me know
That you are mad at me
For doing something stupid
To you
After we hang up
I delete your phone number
From my phone logs
And I try and forget
That sometimes
I hate my life
And that sometimes
I hate what I do too
I alienate myself
And others too
I try to be
A positive reasonable man
But I end up
Acting like
A suicidal teenage boy

Late at night
I realize that
I am sometimes a fuck up
And then I think
That everyone
Must be a fuck up
At sometime in their life
This consoles me a little
But I still
Sometimes hate my life
And what I do
But deep down inside

I know
I know I am a good person
And that I mean well
Even when I push you away
I know
I know that I do good work
Maybe
Just maybe I am meant
To work alone

#1600

Loud Realization

When I was about 25
I really really hated my life
And what was going on around me
I figured that I was paying
For being a lousy kid
Until I was 18 years old
(Well maybe until I was 21...anyways...)
So that the next
18 years of my life
Would be horrible
And that when
I turned 36
Everything would change

From 19 to 35 years were hell for me
Finding out that I had Schizophrenia
Suffering from chronic depression
Losing high school friends
As well as losing my Grandfather Hamilton
Were terrible punishment
At least that is what I thought it was
Flashback to last summer when I was 35
It was like a switch was flicked
I started selling paintings
And getting <u>paying</u> photography gigs
And to top it all off
I was/am surrounded by great people

I have come to the realization
That from here on in
Everything will only get better
My work/art
My family
My friends

Maybe even a lover
Maybe even getting even more
Comfortable with myself and who I am
And finally believing
In myself and that
Everything will work out,
Finally, for the better

To quote Crass
One of my favorite bands
"The problems that you suffer from
Are the problems that you make
The shit we have to climb through
Is the shit we choose to take
If you don't like the life you live
Change it now it's your's"
So maybe just maybe
It was <u>NOT</u> punishment
It was a poor outlook on life
I finally feel that it has changed, and now
Ain't life grand?!

> this piece was written at 1:25 PM
> on February 19, 2008
> in Edmonton

Technical information for the "25 Days" photography project. The camera used for this project was a Mamiya 23 Standard 6x7 & a Mamiya Sekor 90mm/F3.5 lens. This was a manual focus camera made circa 1964.

page #135 - July 17/06: Fuji Provia 100F/120 cross processed
Page #136 - July 18/06: Fuji NPS 160/120
Page #137 - July 19/06: Fuji NPH 400/120
Page #138 - July 20/06: Kodak E200/120 cross processed
Page #139 - July 21/06: Fuji NHG 2 800/120
Page #140 - July 22/06: AGFA Optima 400/120
Page #141 - July 23/06: Kodak Portra 160VC/120
Page #142 - July 24/06: Kodak Portra 400NC/120
Page #143 - July 25/06: Kodak Portra 400UC/120
Page #144 - July 26/06: Kodak Portra 800/120
Page #145 - July 27/06: Fuji Provia 100F/120 cross processed
Page #146 - July 28/06: Fuji Provia 100F/120 cross processed
Page #147 - July 29/06: Fuji Provia 100F/120 cross processed
Page #148 - July 30/06: Fuji Provia 100F/120 cross processed
Page #149 - July 31/06: AGFA Optima 400/120
Page #150 - Aug 1/06: Kodak Portra 400UC/120
Page #151 - Aug 2/06: AGFA Optima 400/120
Page #152 - Aug 3/06: Kodak Portra 400NC/120
Page #153 - Aug 4/06: Kodak Portra 160VC/220
Page #154 - Aug 5/06: Kodak Portra 160VC/220
Page #155 - Aug 6/06: Kodak Portra 160VC/220
Page #156 - Aug 7/06: Kodak Portra 160VC/220
Page #157 - Aug 8/06: Kodak Portra 160VC/220
Page #158 - Aug 9/06: Kodak Portra 160VC/220
Page #159 - Aug 10/06: Kodak Portra 160VC/220

You can see most of these photographs in colour at
www.dramaticsituations.com

In Loving Memory

Mary Lois Hamilton
Born:
March 9, 1922
Oakburn, Manitoba

Passed Away:
May 19, 2008
Shoal Lake, Manitoba

Mary is survived by:

Sons: Larry (Lynne), Rick Marion, Ken (Marjorie), Allen (Wanda); Daughter Judith.

Sisters: Margaret, Phyllis, Ruth, Shirley (Bill), and Zetta (Wayne). Mary is also survived by eight grandchildren, and two great grandchildren.

Mary was predeceased by parents John and Ethel Black, brother Douglas, husband Ronald, brothers-in-law Joe Menzies, Weldon "Red" McIntosh, and Gordon McIntyre.

Saturday, May 24, 2008 at 2:00 p.m.
Rossburn Community Church

Processional Hymn #398: I Come to the Garden A
Welcome and Announcements
Scripture Reading
Piano Solo: Marjorie Hamilton, You Raise Me U
Eulogy
Hymn #365: I am Weak but Thou Art Strong
Message
Prayers of the People and the Lord's Prayer
Benediction
Recessional Hymn #32: How Great Thou Art

There will be a time for lunch and fellowship in the basement Rossburn Community Church following the interment at Rossburn Municipal Cemetery.

Officiant
Russ Andrew

Organist
Wendell Cleland

Pallbearers
Colin Hamilton ~ Aaron Hamilton ~ Corey Hamilton
Mickey Heneghan ~ Wayne Carson ~ Clint Pelletier

On behalf of the family we would like to extend our deepest gratitude for all the kindness and support.

Rae's Funeral Service in care of arrangements

Dedicated with love to the memory of:
MARY LOIS HAMILTON
March 9th, 1922
May 19th, 2008

Thanks.

www.ingramcontent.com/pod-product-compliance
Lightning Source LLC
Chambersburg PA
CBHW070058020526
44112CB00034B/1436